# A Teacher's Guide

by Al Balmer

Drawings by Mike Harnisch

Edited by Chris Cotter

## Doc Fizzix Publishing Company

Round Rock, Texas

If you have questions or comments about material in this book, I will be glad to answer them.  Please call or write:

# Doc Fizzix

## 1809 Laurel Path
## Round Rock, TX 78664

## (512) 218-0454

## http://www.docfizzix.com

Alden J. Balmer is Doc Fizzix

Third Edition

ISBN 0-9656674-0-5

Printed by
Armstrong Printing
Austin, Texas

# Table of Contents

# Table of Contents

iv

# Table of Contents

# Table of Contents

# SAFE USE OF HAND TOOLS

Hand tools are easy and safe to use when they are used properly. Please inform yourself about safe use of hand tools by reading ahead and by consulting your teacher or mentor. Described below are some commonly used hand tools and some dangerous situations that can result if they are not used properly.

**Safety Glasses** The most important safety aid is inexpensive and available at any hardware store or from your shop teacher.

**Hot Glue Gun** Very useful for quickly fastening different materials together with a reasonably strong bond. Hot glue guns can cause **minor burns** if the gun nozzle or hot glue touches the skin.

**Soldering Iron** Useful for making electrical connections. Soldering irons can cause **minor burns** if the soldering tip, or hot solder, touches the skin.

**Electric Hand Drill** Hand drills are useful for placing holes in materials and might be used in the fabrication of wheels, for example. **Wear safety glasses.** If too much force is applied, drill bits can break, launching fragments into the air. Material removed by the drill bit can also become airborne. Students using hand drills should work a safe distance from students who are not wearing safety glasses. **Clamp work securely.** A spinning drill bit can grab the workplace and yank it around if it is not properly clamped in place, resulting in injuries, especially if the workplace has sharp edges. A small vice or clamp is useful for this purpose. **Note what is underneath the piece being drilled.** Be sure that drilling is done into a secure block of scrap wood or into a clear space.

**Hacksaw** Hacksaws are useful for cutting a variety of materials. **Wear safety glasses.** Removed material could become airborne. **Keep hands away from the cutting zone.** The blade can jump and cause minor hand injuries. **Clamp work securely.** This removes any inclination to hold the workplace near the cutting zone and allows better control of the tool.

**Wire Clippers** These tools are useful for cutting wire and thin shafts. If both sides of the piece are not securely held, it may shoot out. Orient the tool so that the section being clipped is aimed at the floor or held in some other way.

**Utility or "Exacto" Knives** Useful for cutting cardboard, foamboard, etc.
**Cut away from yourself** (i.e., don't draw the blade towards your hand or any other part of your body). **Store tools safely.** Avoid leaving exposed blades on table surfaces. Use a handle with a retractable blade if possible.

# Acknowledgments

I dedicate this book to my mother, Dr. Karen Ostlund, who has so unselfishly given her love to me. Without her help I would never be where I am today.

A special thanks goes to Mark Daniels and David Hailes for all their help and ideas in the making of this book. Mark and David teach at McNeil High School in Round Rock, Texas. Mark teaches mathematics and David teaches science. It is their dedication to their subject matters that I envy the most. They are truly the best in their profession.

# About the Author

Alden J. Balmer is an award-winning physics teacher at McNeil High School in the Round Rock Independent School District, located in Round Rock Texas. His mouse trap car competitions have helped increase the physics enrollment at McNeil High School from one class of 15 students to 10 classes of 25 students. In 1996, Al Balmer was selected as the most outstanding science teacher in the State of Texas; this was in part because of his creative approach to teaching science and his ability to hook students into science with creative engineering projects such as the mouse trap car competition. Al Balmer and his students have appeared on locally and nationally aired television programs and at national science conventions, discussing how to build and race mouse-trap cars. In this book, Al Balmer (Doc Fizzix) discusses all the important elements that need to be considered in order to construct the perfect mouse trap car. From reading this book you will also learn the basic conceptual concepts that are needed to construct your own mouse trap car and how those concepts relate to mouse trap car engineering. Al Balmer has built over 100 different mouse trap vehicles and extensively tested each car to determine the important variables that needed to be considered in order to achieve maximum performance.

# About the Illustrator

Mike Harnisch is a published cartoonist and freelance artist. His cartoons have appeared in the *Austin American-Statesman, The Daily Texan*, and several other national and local publications. He created his cartoon character, "Fred," at the age of 8, and has been drawing ever since. Mike's ultimate dream is to become a syndicated cartoonist, and his hard work and perseverance thus far may help him realize that dream. In 1996, Mike's cartoon, "Wet Feet," helped him earn the National College Media award for Best Cartoon Strip and he continues to draw daily and weekly strips along with illustrations. Mike lives in Austin, Texas and loves the Beatles, the Buffalo Bills, and Erin, his girlfriend.

# What is a **Mouse-Trap Car** and How does it **Work?**

A mouse-trap car is a vehicle that is designed to run on the energy that can be stored in a wound up mouse-trap spring. The most basic design is to attach a string to a mouse-trap's lever arm. This string is wound around a drive axle as the mouse-trap lever arm is set. Once the mouse-trap's arm is released, the mouse-trap's arm pulls the string off the drive axle causing the drive axle and the wheels to rotate, propelling the vehicle. This basic design can propel a vehicle several meters for any first-time builder. In order to build extreme distance vehicles that travel over **100 meters** or extreme speed cars that travel **5 meters in a second,** you must understand how each of the different variables individually affect the performance of a mouse-trap car. For example, how does the wheel size affect the overall distance your vehicle can travel? How does the length of the mouse-trap's lever arm affect the speed at which your vehicle can travel? By reading each section of this book you will learn about the different variables that affect your vehicle's performance. By reading each section of this book you will also learn how to modify each variable to build a top performing distance or speed vehicle.

**Getting Started**

**Why build a mouse-trap car?** Building mouse-trap cars allows you to experience the process of design first-hand. When you design your vehicle, you have to start with some ideas and then turn them into real-life models that work. Building mouse-trap cars is an advanced form of problem solving with two main ingredients:

*1.* **You don't know what the problems are.** *Many of the problems in building a mouse-trap car will be discovered and solved as you go along; each person's challenges will be different.*

*2.* **There is never one right answer!**

One last thought before you get started. Throughout the construction of your car, you will have to deal with tradeoffs. For example, building a car for greater performance usually means sacrificing fuel efficiency. When applying any of the ideas and hints in this book to the construction of your car, understand that an extreme exaggeration of any one idea may have a negative effect on the performance of your vehicle. **It is best to find a harmonious combination among all ideas through repeated experimentation.** Experimentation is essential to maximum performance. Experiment often and early, and don't worry about making mistakes. Keep in mind you will not know many of the problems until you encounter them. Engineering is a process by which ideas are tested and re-tested in an effort to produce the best working product. A good engineer knows one way to get something to work and 99 ways it won't work. **Do not be afraid to try your different ideas; your tested ideas will lead you to success!** Also, by understanding the basic conceptual physics concepts presented in this book, you will be able to make good decisions about building the perfect car. **Don't delay, get started!**

Almost any materials can be used in the construction of a good mouse-trap car.  It is up to the designer to determine the appropriate application of such materials.  Sizes, lengths, diameters, widths, and kinds of materials are more-or-less left up to the designer.  The human imagination is a wonderful gift, and our own ingenuity allows us to take ordinary objects with functions different from what were intended and turn them into components of a working machine.  For example, a compact disc is a good device for storing information and playing it back, but it also makes a great wheel. Good luck!

## Tools of the Trade

- *Dremel Tool*
- *Hobby Knife*
- *Files*
  - *Round*
  - *Square*
  - *Knife*
- *Power Drill*
- *Drill Bits*
- *Glue*
  - *Super Glue*
  - *Wood Glue*
  - *Hot Glue*
  - *Rubber Cement*
- *Coping Saw or Hack Saw*
- *Pliers*

**Getting Started**

MOTION

FRICTION

A ball rolling across the floor eventually slows to a stop. The reason the ball slows to a stop is because of **friction**. Friction is a force that opposes motion and always is in a direction opposite to the motion of an object. An object that slides to the right experiences friction towards the left. If it was not for friction, the ball would roll forever, as long as there was nothing—like a wall—to stop its motion. Your mouse-trap car is affected by friction in the same way as the rolling ball is. Friction occurs anytime two surfaces slip, slide, or move against one another. There are two basic types of friction—**surface friction** and **fluid friction**. In some situations fluid friction is called air resistance. A ball falling through the air is affected by fluid friction and a block sliding on a table is mainly affected by surface friction as well as a little air resistance. **The greater the amount of friction between two surfaces, the larger the force that will be required to keep an object moving**. In order to overcome friction, a constant force is needed. In order to maintain a constant force, there must be a supply of **energy**. A ball which is given an initial push will roll until all its energy is consumed by friction, at which point it will roll to a stop. The smaller the forces

CHEESE

TABLE

**4**

**Friction**

of friction acting against a moving object (like a ball or mouse-trap car), the farther it will travel on its available energy supply. **Eliminating all forms of friction is the key to success no matter what type of vehicle you are building.**

**Surface friction** occurs between any two surfaces that touch or rub against one another. The cause of surface friction is mutual contact of irregularities between the touching surfaces. The irregularities act as obstructions to motion. Even surfaces that appear to be very smooth are irregular when viewed microscopically. Luckily, during motion surface friction is **unaffected by the relative speed** of the contacting surfaces. Even though the speed of an object may increase, the force of surface friction will remain constant. This means that the same force is required to slide an object at a slow or fast rate of speed on a given surface. **The amount of friction acting between two surfaces depends on the kinds of material from which the two surfaces are made and how hard the surfaces are pressed together.** Ice is more slippery than concrete; therefore, ice has less friction or less resistance to slippage. A heavier brick is harder to push and has more friction than a lighter brick only because the heavier brick is pushed with more force into the ground.

**Friction**

FRICTION
POINTS BETWEEN
AXLE AND FRAME

Minimizing surface friction on your mouse-trap car will allow its wheels to spin more freely, resulting in a car that travels faster, farther and wastes less energy. **The most common area where surface friction will occur is between the axle and the chassis.** The interface between the axle and the chassis is called the **bearing**. A **plain bearing** can be as simple as an axle in a drilled hole. A **bushing** is a smooth sleeve placed in a hole that gives the axle a smother rubbing surface, which means less surface friction. Some combinations of material should not be used because they do not help the cause. For example, avoid using aluminum as the axle or the bearing sleeve. A **ball bearing** is a set of balls in the hole which is arranged so that the axle rolls on the balls instead of sliding in a sleeve. A rolling ball has very little friction; therefore, ball bearings usually provide the best performance. Ball bearings have the least friction, but they are the most expensive, so you must evaluate your budget when thinking about ball bearings. You can buy small ball bearings at a local hobby store that deals with remote-controlled vehicles.

AXLE

BUSHING

BUSHING COLLAR

ROLLER BALLS

BALL BEARING

BALL BEARING

**Friction**

6

# Mounting a Ball Bearing In the Frame

BALL BEARING

SMOKE

DREMEL BURNS HOLE IN WOOD

7

BALL BEARING SHOULD FIT EASILY INTO THE DREMELED-OUT HOLE

*If you do not have a dremel tool, you can use a **drill** bit that matches the size of the bearing. Be carful since large drill bits can tear up the wooden frame causing the wood to **splinter**. Wrap a piece of tape around the area to be drilled in order to help protect the wood from **splintering**.*

**Friction**

# Construction Tip

# Making A Bushing

**STEP ONE**

FIND A PIECE OF BRASS TUBING THAT IS TWO SIZES LARGER THAN YOUR AXLE

BRASS TUBING (2 SIZES LARGER)

AXLE

THEY SHOULD SLIDE TOGETHER EFFORTLESSLY AS SHOWN

**STEP TWO**

JEWELER'S SAW

BRASS TUBING

USING A JEWELER'S SAW, CUT OFF A PIECE OF THE BRASS TUBING. BE **SURE** THAT THE CUT IS PERPENDICULAR

**STEP THREE**

ROUGH EDGES

FILE

BUSHING

USE A METAL FILE TO CLEAN UP THE ROUGH EDGES, MAKING THE BUSHING EASY TO FIT AXLE INTO

**STEP FOUR**

BUSHING

GLUE THE BUSHING INTO THE WOOD AND SLIDE AXLE THROUGH

AXLE

**Friction**

**Lubrications** help moving parts slide against each other with less energy loss by reducing the surface friction. Try a quick experiment. Rub your hands together lightly and quickly. You should notice that your hands become warmer. This is because the friction between your hands turns some of the input energy into heat. Heat is lost or wasted energy in many moving machines. Put a small amount of hand lotion onto your hands and try the experiment again. Notice that your hands do not become as hot and it is easier to move them against one another. Different **lubricants** work better with different materials. Oils and greases are used between most metal-on-metal parts. Oils do not work well between metal and wood, but graphite powder does. With your mouse-trap car, it is best to try different lubricants and observe their effects. WD-40®, Dura-Lube®, Slick 50®, and graphite are necessary materials for your tool box.

# Brain Tip

**A SECRET TIP FROM DOC FIZZIX:** *Do not use lubricants with ball bearings. Soak ball bearings in rubbing alcohol in order to remove all grease residue from within the bearing. Although lubricants prevent wear and in some cases reduce the overall force of friction, with slow moving mouse-trap cars lubricants actually increase the friction. The reason that lubricants do not work at low speeds has to do with the cohesive forces of the lubricant. At low speeds lubricants are actually sticky and stick to themselves, requiring larger forces to break free and move.*

SPIN A BEARING ON A PENCIL TO REMOVE GREASE AFTER SOAK- ING IN ALCOHOL.

9

**Friction**

Friction is not restricted to solids sliding over one another. Friction also occurs in liquids and gases, collectively called **fluids**. Just as the friction between solid surfaces depends on the nature of the surfaces, **fluid friction** depends on the nature of the fluid. For example, friction is greater in water than it is in air. But unlike the friction between solid surfaces, fluid friction does **depend on speed and area of contact**. This makes sense, for the amount of fluid pushed aside by a boat or airplane depends on the size and the shape of the craft. A slow-moving boat or airplane encounters less friction than fast-moving boats or airplanes. Wide boats and airplanes must push aside more fluid than narrower crafts. If the flow of fluid is relatively smooth, the friction force is approximately proportional to the speed of

A TEAR DROP IS THE MOST AERODYNAMIC SHAPE, CUTTING THROUGH THE AIR WITH THE LEAST AMOUNT OF AIR RESISTANCE, MUCH LIKE THE WING OF AN AIRPLANE.

the object. Above a critical speed this simple proportion breaks down as fluid flow becomes erratic and friction increases dramatically.

**The amount of air friction or fluid friction depends on the speed and the shape of a moving object**. The faster an object moves, the more collisions that occur with particles of the fluid, causing increased friction. The shape of a moving object, its **aerodynamic,** determines the **ease of flow** of the fluid around the moving object. Fast cars are designed and shaped to cut through the air with less friction so they can move faster. Trucks have a special cowling that increases their aerodynamics and allows air to flow more easily over the trailer. Increased aerodynamics saves energy. Fish have aerodynamic shapes that allow them to move through the water with

**Friction**

less effort. Keep in mind that there are situations in which you would want to increase the air resistance. A good example is the use of a parachute on a dragster to help it stop the vehicle or the flaps on an airplane to help slow it down.

Because the force of **air resistance** increases as the speed of an object increases, faster moving mouse-

BEFORE

AFTER

USING SAND PAPER, YOU CAN RESHAPE SURFACES, DECREASING FLUID FRICTION.

trap cars will have more air resistance acting against them, causing them to use more energy and come to rest sooner than a similarly built slower-moving mouse-trap car. Keeping this in mind, good aerodynamics will improve performance of any vehicle, no matter what type of car you are building. This means that your car must be smooth with few points of **air drag**. Inspect the body for flat surfaces on leading edges that could catch air, thus increasing the air drag. Rounding the

l e a d i n g edges of y o u r v e h i c l e w i l l a l l o w f o r smoother movement of air around your

MORE SURFACE AREA EQUALS LESS PRESSURE AND MORE AIR RESISTANCE BUT NO INCREASE IN TRACTION

vehicle. Cars made from wood need to be sanded smooth. **Sanding** will remove any unwanted irregularities, thus decreasing the force of air resistance acting on your car once it is in motion. Tires should be thin. Thin tires are more aerodynamic and slice through the air more smoothly. Wider tires will have more air drag than narrower t i r e s . Therefore, try to pick thin tires when you are building your mouse-trap car.

LESS SURFACE AREA EQUALS MORE PRESSURE ARE LESS AIR RESISTANCE BUT NO DECREASE IN TRACTION

## Friction

# Experiment

FORCE ON HAND

DIRECTION OF MOTION

*To see how much force the air can have, try the following* **experiment** *next time you are in a car. Carefully hold your hand out the window. Try holding your hand so that your thumb points toward the sky and then try holding your hand so that your thumb point towards the direction of travel. You will have a better understanding of* **fluid friction** *after this experiment.*

FORCE ON HAND

DIRECTION OF MOTION

LEAST AMOUNT OF AIR RESISTANCE

SMALL FORCE

DIRECTION OF MOTION

**Friction**

# Thrust Washers

When building your car, it is best to glue the axles in place so that they do not have a side-to-side movement. In some situations it may be difficult to prevent an axle from moving side-to-side, in which case you will want to use a thrust washer or spacer. **Thrust washers** can be used to eliminate the rubbing friction of a wheel touching the frame.

THRUST WASHER

UNWANTED FRICTION

WHEEL

If a wheel has a side-to-side movement, a thrust washer can be used to prevent the wheel from moving into the frame and rubbing, causing poor performance of your vehicle.

13

## Experiment

*Try an experiment to learn about a **thrust bearing**. Place a book on the table and give it a spin. The book should spin slowly and then stop quickly. Now place a coin under the book and give it a spin again. The book should spin for a considerably longer time before stopping.*

SPIN

PENNY IS PLACED UNDERNEATH BOOK

**Friction**

The number of wheels your vehicle has does not have an effect on the overall friction. Vehicles with three wheels will often have fewer friction points than vehicles with four wheels. However, the **distribution of weight** for a three wheeled vehicle is spread out over three wheels rather than four; therefore, there is more pressure on the turning points and an increase in friction for each point. The decease in the number of **friction points** is offset by the increase in **pressure**. This is what we call "a wash." You get no change! No matter the number of wheels, the total amount of friction should be the same. The advantage of using fewer wheels is better wheel alignment. With three-wheeled cars, it will be easier to adjust the steering of the vehicle because there are fewer wheels to be aligned.

MOST
ENERGY
EFFICIENT

ENERGY
LOST

FRICTION
CAUSES
TURN

**14**

## Steering Alignment

Building a vehicle that travels straight can be somewhat challenging, especially when building a long traveling distance vehicle where any small misalignment in the wheels is exaggerated over a long distance. If your car does not travel straight, energy is being wasted. Vehicles turn because of one reason: **"THE WHEELS ARE NOT POINTING IN THE SAME DIRECTION!"** What does wheel alignment have to do with friction? Vehicles turn because wheels use friction to push a vehicle into a turn. For example, if a wheel is turned so that it points to the left, the ground actually pushes the car in this direction. If the frictional force is not large enough to overcome the **momentum** of the vehicle (like a car traveling fast

**Friction**

# Construction Tip

THE RIGHT SIDE OF THE FRAME IS TOO LONG, CAUSING THE AXLE TO BE CROOKED, MISALIGNING THE CAR

CUT THE SHORT PIECE

GLUE OR TAPE A PIECE OF WOOD FOR SUPPORT

on ice), the vehicle does not make the turn. When building your vehicle, be aware of your wheel alignment. If your car turns you have to change the alignment of the wheels in the direction opposite the turn. Sometimes on a big-wheeled vehicle the **string tension** can pull an axle out of alignment, so always test your car under operating conditions. **Do not just push your vehicle to see if it travels straight.**

15

## Another Idea to Get You Going Straight

BY MOVING A DRILL SIDE TO SIDE, YOU CAN "WARBLE" THE AXLE HOLE, THEN USE CLAY TO CUSTOMIZE

CLAY

TOP VIEW

AXLE

USING THIS TECHNIQUE, YOU CAN FIND THE PERFECT POSITION FOR YOUR AXLE

**Friction**

*Once the vehicle travels straight, squirt **glue** around the hole in order to hold the axle in place.*

# Wheel Size

You should consider the **diameter** of the wheels in the construction of your distance vehicle. The number of turns a wheel makes has an effect on the energy consumed by a wheel. Large diameter wheels will make fewer turns over the same distance compared to smaller diameter wheels, thus reducing the total amount of energy needed to overcome friction.

Larger wheels do not decrease the *amount* of friction, only *how far* the friction acts. **Energy**, or **work**, is equal to the force times the distance over which the force is applied. If the force of friction is applied over a smaller turning distance compared to vehicle travel distance, less energy will be wasted due to friction, which leaves more energy to move the car.

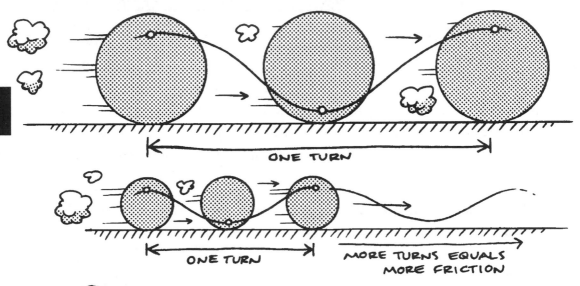

ONE TURN

ONE TURN

MORE TURNS EQUALS MORE FRICTION

*With distance vehicles, you want the smallest possible force acting over the longest possible distance; therefore, you want to build a car with a small axle to a large wheel ratio. A small axle with a large wheel will cover more distance per each turn of the axle when compared to a smaller wheel size with the same axle.*

**Friction**

# Making a **Big** Wheel

FIRST, MOUNT THE LARGE FOAM- "ALMOST ROUND" WHEEL BETWEEN TWO LARGE WASHERS USING A NUT AND BOLT

SECOND, PLACE THE WHEEL AND BOLT ASSEMBLY INTO THE END OF A POWER DRILL... MAKE SURE IT IS **SECURE**.

RAZOR MUST **NOT FACE UP**

THIRD, HAVE SOMEONE HOLD THE DRILL TIGHTLY ON THE EDGE OF A TABLE WHILE YOU USE A RAZOR TO "SHAVE" WHEEL

FINALLY, REMOVE MASS FROM THE WHEEL USING AN EKACTO KNIFE TO DECREASE INERTIA

**17**

## Brain Tip

**Compact discs** *can make great wheels for mouse-trap cars. Finally there is a use for all of those online disks you keep getting in the mail!*

**Friction**

Friction is not always a bad thing. **Without friction you could not move anywhere**. As you walk forward, it is the friction on the bottom of your feet that allows for the grip you need to move. It is the friction between the road and your tires that keeps the wheels from slipping and allows your vehicle to move. This type of friction is called **traction** and is a desired form of friction. What type of wheels work best: fat tires, thin tires, knobby tires, or smooth tires? Knobby tires have good traction if the road surface is rough, but the tradeoff is that they are inefficient and use more energy than smooth wheels. When

COMPRESSED KNOBS APPLY EXTRA PRESSURE WHICH GENERATES MORE HEAT, WASTING ENERGY

pressure is placed directly on a knob, more force compresses the tire causing the rubber and air inside the tire to heat up. The energy it takes to compress the rubber and air in the tire is lost as heat.

Knobby tires become hotter with continued use. Race cars use smooth tires called **slicks**. Smooth wheels will be more energy efficient and allow a car to travel faster. On mouse-trap cars, smooth tires will allow a vehicle to travel a longer distance.

The amount of **grip** your tires have on the floor not only depends on whether you have knobby tires or slicks but also depends on the material your tires are made from and the force

**Friction**

# Brain Tip

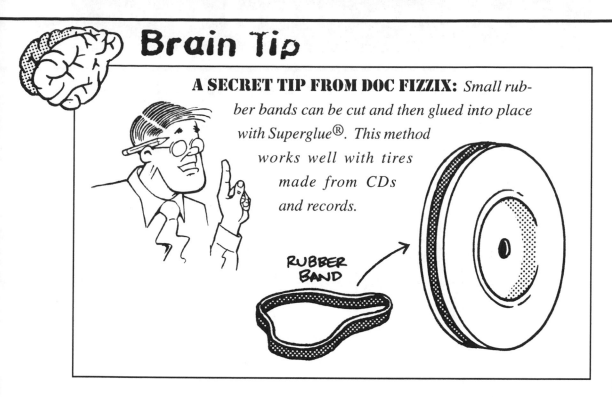

**A SECRET TIP FROM DOC FIZZIX:** *Small rubber bands can be cut and then glued into place with Superglue®. This method works well with tires made from CDs and records.*

RUBBER BAND

pushing the tires to the floor. Different compounds of materials will have different amounts of grip. For instance, rubber bands wrapped around a wooden wheel will provide better grip during acceleration than the wood of the wheel will alone. **You should select or design tires to provide maximum traction or grip on the floor**. Tires with little grip on the floor will have a tendency to slip when under a load, thereby decreasing your car's maximum acceleration or distance. You can also increase the traction by adding a non-slipping gel like **Traction Action®**, a sticky gel that is smeared on the wheels. Experiment with different materials in order to find the best traction.

GLUE

COMPACT DISK

RUBBER BAND

**Friction**

## Newton's First **Law** of Motion:

*Every material object continues in its state of rest or in uniform motion in a straight line unless it is compelled to change that state by forces acting on it.*

**20**

**Inertia** is just a fancy word that means **resistance to change**. **Mass** is the numerical measurement of inertia. **Weight** is related to mass and inertia but weight is not the same thing. Weight is a product of the amount of mass an object has and the amount of gravity pulling on the mass. An example of the difference can be understood using a bowling ball. On earth you can feel the weight of a bowling ball as you hold it to your side. If you held the bowling ball on the moon, it would feel a lot lighter than on the earth. This is because the gravity on the moon is not as strong as the gravity on the earth; therefore, the weight of the bowling ball is less than its weight on the earth. Now if you compared throwing the bowling ball down the bowling lane on the earth and on the moon you would find that there is no apparent difference in force or feel. This is because the mass of the bowling ball is the same in each location and by throwing the bowling ball you are working against its inertia—not its weight.

## Inertia, Force, Acceleration

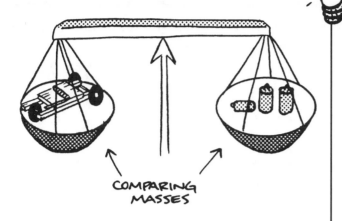

COMPARING MASSES

**Mass** and **weight** are measured differently. Mass is measured on a balance by **comparing** known masses to an unknown mass. Weight is measured with a scale where **gravity** can pull on the object. Wherever you go in the universe, your measurement of mass will not change, but your measurement of weight will change depending on the pull of gravity in your location.

SCALE

WEIGHING — NOT COMPARING — MEASURES THE **PULL** BETWEEN THE OBJECT AND THE EARTH (GRAVITY)

*Objects resist change in motion. Simply put, things tend to keep on doing whatever they are already doing. This is Newton's First Law of Motion which is often called the* **Law of Inertia.**

**Inertia, Force, Acceleration**

# Experiment

A good way to learn about **inertia** is the following experiment. Place some old dishes and plates on top of a smooth table cloth. With a quick tug, pull the table cloth off the table! **Do not pull up on the table cloth but pull outward.** This demonstrates that objects at rest tend to stay at rest. This experiment will work better with food on the plates and in the bowls.

TADA!

## Inertia, Force, Acceleration

# Newton's Second Law

*If you want to change the motion of an object, you have to apply a* **force**. *Net forces cause objects to accelerate or change their state of motion. Newton recognized that his first law needed some additional explanation because most of the motion we observe around us undergoes changes and is the result of one or more applied forces; therefore,* **Newton wrote a Second Law of Motion which relates force, mass, and acceleration.**

## Newton's Second Law of Motion:

*The acceleration of an object is directly proportional to the net force acting on the object (in the direction of the net force) and is inversely proportional to the mass of the object.*

Simply put, **mass resists change or acceleration, and force causes acceleration**. If you want to double the acceleration of an object, you have to double the pulling or pushing force. If you can't increase the force and you still want to increase the acceleration, then you have to **remove mass** (e.g., cut the original mass in half if you want to double the acceleration).

## Inertia, Force, Acceleration

When you build your car, Newton's laws remind you of the following: **mass is resistance to change!** Therefore, more massive vehicles will require more force and energy to start moving when compared to less massive vehicles. Whether building a speed car or distance car, **it is best to build the lightest vehicle possible**. Vehicles that are light will not only be easier to start moving but will also have less friction acting on the bearings than heavier vehicles will. Because the frame of your car rests directly on its bearings, heavier frames will press on the bearings with greater force, causing the bearings to grind more than on a lighter frame. Be careful since a car that is too light will not have enough traction to accelerate quickly. Somewhere between too heavy and too light is the perfect amount of mass for your vehicle, and only through experimentation will you find your target mass. In the process of finding your ideal mass, it is best to remove as much mass as possible because you can always add mass to strategic locations later to improve performance. Think about Newton's laws when you are building your car. **Mass works against acceleration. Remove as much mass as possible!** Force causes acceleration. If you need more pulling force, you can shorten the lever arm and move the mouse trap closer to the drive wheels. Shortening the lever arm implies moving the string closer to the hinge on the mouse-trap.

LESS FORCE

MORE FORCE

*Adjust the **pulling force** by attaching the string to different points on the lever arm. When you change the string attachment point, you must also adjust the position of the mouse-trap from the pulling axle.*

## Inertia, Force, Acceleration

# Construction Tip

**A SECRET TIP FROM DOC FIZZIX:** *The one secret that I can share with you that will most improve your car's performance is the following:* **RE-MOVE MASS FROM YOUR WHEELS.** *By cutting out sections of the wheels, your wheels will require less force and energy to turn and accelerate. You can also improve performance by removing mass from the frame*

COMPACT DISK

DREMEL TOOL

LESS MASS = LESS INERTIA

DRILL

**Inertia, Force, Acceleration**

25

The mouse trap only exerts a force where you direct it to exert a force. String is often used to transfer a force from one point to another. **Choosing the proper string is critical.** If you use a string that cannot handle the pulling force, it will snap as you release the mouse trap. If you use a string that is too thick, it will not wind around the drive axle smoothly, causing the pulling force to be inconsistent. **DO NOT USE THREAD.** Use **Kevlar®**-braided fishing string, not the plastic-type fishing string. Kevlar®-braided fishing string is the best string to use because it does not stretch and can wind around a small axle without tangling. Kevlar®-braided fishing line is extremely strong and thin so that it will not break or get tangled while unwinding from the axle. The string must not be tied to the axle. If the string is tied to the axle, it will begin to rewind itself and will cause your car to come to a sudden stop. String **slippage** during the acceleration of your vehicle can be eliminated by a **hook-like device** attached to the car's axle on which a looped string or hook can be attached.

STRING LENGTH SHOULD BE A BIT SHORTER THAN THE DISTANCE FROM THE LEVER ARM TO THE DRIVE AXLE. THIS WILL ALLOW THE LOOP TO RELEASE FROM THE HOOK, PREVENTING THE STRING FROM REWINDING.

*Use **NO MORE** string than the length required to reach the pulling axle when the trap is in the relaxed position.*

## Inertia, Force, Acceleration

# Construction Tip

## Making the Perfect Loop Knot

**STEP ONE**

FOLD A SMALL PART OF THE STRING OVER ITSELF TO FORM A LOOP

STRING (KEVLAR IS RECOMMENDED)

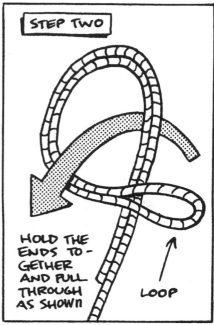

**STEP TWO**

HOLD THE ENDS TOGETHER AND PULL THROUGH AS SHOWN

LOOP

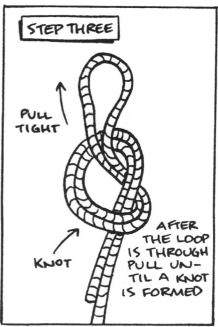

**STEP THREE**

PULL TIGHT

KNOT

AFTER THE LOOP IS THROUGH PULL UNTIL A KNOT IS FORMED

**STEP FOUR**

YES! IT'S *THAT* EASY!

**Inertia, Force, Acceleration**

# Construction Tip

## Making an Axle Hook

STEP ONE

DRILL, OR DREMEL TOOL

DRIVE AXLE

DRILL A HOLE INTO THE DRIVE AXLE

STEP TWO

SMALL TUBE

GLUE

GLUE A SMALL BRASS TUBE INTO THE AXLE HOLE

STEP THREE

AXLE TURN

STRING

STEP FOUR

STRING SHOULD WIND TIGHT AND UNTANGLED

*In order to achieve **maximum performance** from your mouse-trap car, it is important that the pulling string does not **slip off** the drive axle **prematurely**. A **release hook** can be constructed to allow the string to remain connected to the axle during the pulling phase and then release once the pulling has stopped. There are two different ways presented in this book to make a good axle hook. The first method is to drill a small hole into the drive axle and then attach a small splint to act as a hook. The second method is to wrap a small piece of wire around the drive axle, twist and glue it in place, and then trim the wire. In either example, if the hook is too long, it may snag the string and not properly release it from the drive axle.*

## Inertia, Force, Acceleration

# Making an Axle Hook

1. TO MAKE AN AXLE HOOK, WRAP A PIECE OF WIRE AROUND THE AXLE. (WIRE THICKNESS SHOULD BE AS *THIN* AS POSSIBLE)

WIRE    DRIVE AXLE

2. GLUE

GLUE HOOK WITH A DAB OF SUPER-GLUE

TWIST WIRE USING NEEDLE-NOSED PLIERS

3. WIRE CUTTERS

MAKE CUT

USE WIRE CUTTERS TO CUT AXLE HOOK CLOSE TO THE DRIVE AXLE

4. THE AXLE HOOK SHOULD BE CENTERED

ALLOW GLUE TO DRY *BEFORE* TESTING WITH STRING

SHORT AXLE HOOK

**29**

**Inertia, Force, Acceleration**

With a distance car, you want to build the **lightest possible vehicle**, although heavy cars can perform well due to their momentum. That is, more massive cars, once moving, will have a greater resistance to change in their motion when

compared to lighter cars. Massive vehicles will tend to maintain their motion, coasting farther than a lighter vehicle (given the same force of friction acting against the vehicle). This is because massive cars can take advantage of what is called **momentum**, which means **inertia in motion**. This sounds like a good idea for building a distance car, but there is a down side to this idea. You have to first get this more massive car moving in order to take advantage of its momentum. Heavy cars will be harder to start because of their inertia, so the pulling force will be larger using more energy at the start to accelerate. In order to increase the **pulling force** you will have to use a shorter lever arm on

your mouse trap. This usually means that the car will not be pulled as far as slower vehicles with longer lever arms. With momentum you are counting on coasting distance, not pulling distance.

The down side is that heavier vehicles will have to travel faster and will therefore experience greater air resistance. This consumes more energy and ultimately the vehicle will not travel as far as a slow moving, energy-conserving vehicle.

MORE FORCE, BUT LESS PULLING DISTANCE

LESS FORCE, BUT MORE PULLING DISTANCE

**Momentum**

30

# Chassis Construction

One obvious consideration in the construction of your mouse-trap car is the **frame** or the **chassis**. The chassis is a mechanical component that must provide structural support for the motor, wheels, axles, etc. It is important that your mouse-trap car's chassis is designed to handle the operations of your vehicle. There are some important tradeoffs that need to be considered. A chassis that is too light may be too delicate to handle the force of a wound up mouse-trap spring. Also, a chassis that is too light will have less weight pushing down on the wheels, causing less tire traction. A chassis that is too heavy will require more energy at the start than a lighter frame. The chassis needs to be **strong** and **stiff**. Strong means that it will not beak under a load. Stiff means it will not bend or has little flex. The first step to a strong, stiff, and light chassis is choosing the right materials. Balsa wood, pine, or bass wood are excellent choices although balsa wood is somewhat brittle and hard to drill holes into without ripping. Other materials can also be used for making a light weight strong and stiff frame. These include **Styrofoam**®, corrugated cardboard, plastics, aluminum and brass tubing.

**Strength**

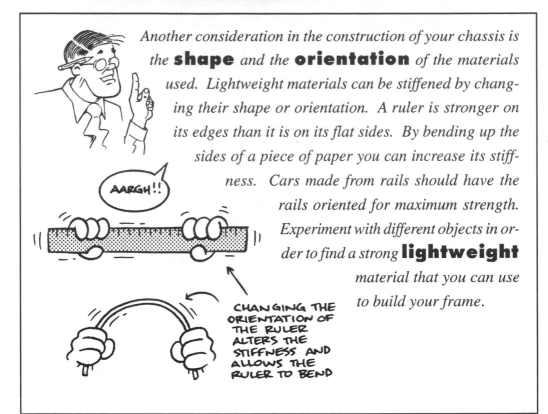

*Another consideration in the construction of your chassis is the* **shape** *and the* **orientation** *of the materials used. Lightweight materials can be stiffened by changing their shape or orientation. A ruler is stronger on its edges than it is on its flat sides. By bending up the sides of a piece of paper you can increase its stiffness. Cars made from rails should have the rails oriented for maximum strength. Experiment with different objects in order to find a strong* **lightweight** *material that you can use to build your frame.*

AARGH!!

CHANGING THE ORIENTATION OF THE RULER ALTERS THE STIFFNESS AND ALLOWS THE RULER TO BEND

# Making a Light-Weight Frame

STEP ONE

TAPE

UNEVEN

EVEN

TAPE TOGETHER TWO STRIPS OF WOOD WITH ONE END LEFT EVEN

STEP TWO

JEWELER'S SAW

CUT OFF UNEVEN WOOD WITH A JEWELER'S SAW OR AN EXACTO SAW

**Strength**

# Construction Tip

**STEP THREE**

PENCIL • RUNG PIECE • PENCIL GUIDE

USE ONE OF THE RUNG PIECES AS A GUIDE FOR CUTTING NOTCHES, WHICH HELP DETERMINE NOTCH THICKNESS

**STEP FOUR**

JEWELER'S SAW • NOTCH CUTS

CUT THE NOTCHES WITH A SAW, GOING HALF-WAY DEEP INTO THE WOOD

**STEP FIVE**

SCREW-DRIVER

USING A SCREWDRIVER OR SHARP TIP, REMOVE WOOD TO FORM A NOTCH

**STEP SIX**

BEFORE REMOVING TAPE, BE SURE TO DRIVE HOLES FOR BOTH AXLES, USING A DRILL OR DREMEL TOOL

DRILL OR DREMEL TOOL

**STEP SEVEN**

PENCIL MARK

USING THE WIDTH OF A MOUSE TRAP, MEASURE AND CUT PIECES OF WOOD TO BE USED AS "RUNGS"

**STEP EIGHT**

USING A SAW, CUT WOOD FROM CORNERS IN ORDER TO FIT RUNG INTO NOTCH

THICKNESS OF FRAME

**STEP NINE**

GLUE • RUNGS

GLUE RUNGS ONTO MAIN FRAME

NOTCH

**STEP TEN**

AXLE HOLE • AXLE

FIT AXLES INTO AXLE HOLES

**Strength**

33

# Center of Mass

**Center of mass** is simply the average position of all particles of mass that make up an object. For symmetric objects of uniform density, such as a ball or a book, this point is usually at the geometrical center. But an irregularly shaped object, such as a baseball bat, will have more mass at one end, causing the center of mass to be located closer to the larger end. If a ball is thrown through the air, it will follow a smooth trajectory. In contrast, if a baseball bat is thrown through the air, it will seem

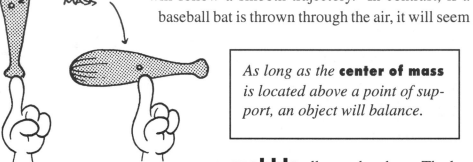

CENTER OF MASS

> *As long as the **center of mass** is located above a point of support, an object will balance.*

to **wobble** all over the place. The bat is actually wobbling around a single point—its center of mass—and that center of mass will follow a smooth trajectory. Objects that are rotating freely tend to rotate so that their center of mass travels smoothly (i.e., most energy efficient) with as little motion as possible. Objects that are forced to rotate around points that are not the center of mass consume more energy.

**Larger wheels are affected more adversely by an offset center of mass than are smaller wheels.** If the center of mass of a large wheel is not in the center of the wheel or through the axle, then the car will tend to wobble through its journey, wasting energy and decreasing the overall distance the car will travel. Also, it is

BEFORE

LIGHTER SIDE

THE CENTER OF MASS (CM) OF THE WHEEL IS NOT IN THE CENTER, CAUSING THE WHEEL TO VIBRATE, WASTING ENERGY

HEAVIER SIDE

possible for a car to **lose distance after stopping and begin rolling backward**; this occurs when the center of mass for a large wheel becomes located in an unstable position. As the center of mass begins to fall towards a more stable position, the wheel begins to rotate, causing the car to move either backward or forward. If the car moves forward, it will gain additional distance after stopping, but there is no way to predict where the center of mass will come to rest when the car stops. For this reason, it is best to **balance** a large wheel, forcing the center of mass to be located through the axle.

Large wheels should be balanced, especially if you have removed material from portions of the wheel in an effort to lighten the car. To balance a wheel, you should hold the wheel by the axle and allow it to turn freely. The heavier side of the wheel will fall towards the bottom. Once the heavier side is marked, mass can be added to the opposite side until the wheel has no tendency to rotate when suspended freely by the axle. Any material can be used to add mass to a large wheel, but **clay** and **pennies** are easy to work with.

AFTER

CM IS NOW IN THE CENTER, ALLOWING THE CAR TO ROLL SMOOTHLY, CONSERVING ENERGY

A PIECE OF CLAY IS USED AS A BALANCE TO PULL CM TOWARD THE CENTER OF ROTATION

## Center of Mass

# Finding the Center of Mass

TACK IS PLACED *AWAY* FROM THE CENTER OF MASS...

AS A RESULT, THE CUT-OUT OF TEXAS WOBBLES AND DOESN'T SPIN AROUND

TO FIND THE CENTER OF MASS, HANG A WEIGHT WITH A PIECE OF STRING...

... AND MARK WHERE IT CROSSES THE CUT-OUT OF TEXAS

MASS

CONTINUE UNTIL SEVERAL LINES CROSS AT ONE POINT (THE CENTER OF MASS)

MARK THE POINT

TACK UP THE CUT OUT AT THE CENTER OF MASS AND IT SHOULD SPIN SMOOTHLY

SPINS SMOOTHLY

**Center of Mass**

# Weight Distribution

Slippage of the drive wheels during the start **wastes energy**. There are several reasons for the slippage problem: not enough traction, too much pulling force or torque, and poor weight distribution. Traction is the grip your wheels have on the floor. You can increase the traction by adding a non-slipping material like a rubber band or Traction Action®, a sticky gel that is smeared on the wheels. If you try adding rubber bands and your car continues to slip on the start, then there are two other components which may be the cause of the problem: **torque** and/or **weight distribution**. If the mouse trap is placed too close to the pulling axle, the wheels will spin on the start. This problem is easy to correct by simply moving the trap away from the pulling axle and extending the lever arm.

RUBBER BAND

IF WHEELS ARE SPINNING ON THE START MOVE THE MOUSE TRAP *AWAY* FROM THE DRIVE AXLE AND EXTEND THE LEVER ARM

SCALES

WEIGHT DIVIDED BY 4, 4 POINTS OF SUPPORT

3 POINTS OF SUPPORT (WEIGHT/3)

*Ideally, the amount of* **traction** *will be greater for a three-wheeled vehicle than a four-wheeled vehicle of same mass and center of mass. Choose your drive wheel(s) based on where more weight is being transferred to the ground.*

## Center of Mass

If the pulling wheels do not have enough traction, the problem may be because of the **distribution of the weight** of the car. Have you ever heard that front-wheel drive cars are better in snow and ice than rear-wheel drive vehicles? Front-wheel drive cars have the engine located directly above the drive wheels; this helps increase the traction on the front wheels. The closer the center of mass is located to the drive wheels, the more traction that will result. The balance point of your car, which represents the center of mass, should be located as close as possible to the drive

CHEESE

DRIVE AXLE

SLIP!

THE WEIGHT IS CENTERED *AWAY* FROM THE DRIVE AXLE WHICH CAUSES SLIPPING

wheels. If your car continues to slip on the start, you may want to try **adding some mass over or near the drive wheels** in order to shift the center of mass towards the drive train.

## Brain Tip

CHEESE

DRIVE AXLE

THE WEIGHT IS CENTERED *NEAR* THE DRIVE AXLE, INCREASING TRACTION

ADDING CLAY ABOVE THE DRIVE AXLE INCREASES TRACTION

DRIVE AXLE

**Center of Mass**

38

# Rotational Inertia

Just as an object at rest tends to stay at rest and an object in motion tends to stay in motion, **an object rotating about an axis tends to remain rotating about the same axis unless an external force or torque acts on it**. The property of an object to resist changes in its rotational state of motion is called **rotational inertia** and is a restatement of Newton's First Law of Motion. **Rotational inertia is the resistance an object has to changes in rotation.** Just as inertia for linear motion depends on the mass of an object, so does rotational inertia. But rotational inertia also depends on one more element—the **location** of the mass with respect to the axis of rotation. The greater the distance between the bulk of an object's mass and its axis of rotation, the greater the rotational inertia. This principle is employed by a weight lifter when he or she twists a barbell with mass located on the ends. When the mass of the barbell is far from the axis of rotation, (i.e., its midpoint), the bar has considerable rotational inertia and is hard to turn or twist. If the mass is placed closer to the center of rotation, the bar twists with less effort. It follows that the greater the rotational inertia of an object, the harder it is to change the rotational state of that object. If rotating, it is difficult to stop; if at rest, it is difficult to rotate.

**39**

## Experiment

*Try an experiment to learn about* **rotational inertia**. *Try twisting a barbell with the weight spaced close together and then far apart. You will definitely get a good feel for rotational inertia after this experiment.*

**Rotational Inertia**

SAME DIAMETER SAME MASS

EASIER TO CHANGE ROTATION

HARD TO CHANGE ROTATION

LESS ROTATIONAL INERTIA BECAUSE MASS IS MORE EVENLY SPREAD OUT FROM CENTER

MORE ROTATIONAL INERTIA BECAUSE MASS IS CONCENTRATED ON THE OUTSIDE, FAR FROM CENTER

Whether you are building a mouse-trap car for speed or distance, it is best to use wheels that have **as little rotational inertia as possible**. The less rotational inertia of your wheels, the less force that is needed to turn or accelerate your wheels. Especially with distance cars, you want to have the smallest possible pulling force. Smaller pulling forces will allow for greater pulling distances. Therefore, **less rotational inertia in the wheels means less required pulling force and greater travel distance** with higher acceleration off the start. Wheels with a large amount of rotational inertia will have a greater coasting distance, but this performance will be offset by the increased amounts of force and energy required to accelerate the vehicle off

the start. **Always pick wheels that are light weight.** Removing mass from the inside of your wheels using a dremel tool or a drill will increase both speed and distance performance. This idea is extremely helpful in an effort to get cars to go faster off the start line or to get them to travel farther using less torque. Store-bought wheels are not always the best solution when determining the wheels for your vehicle. Some of the best wheels are found in your home: old compact discs, Styrofoam®, can lids and tops, records, mat board, or other light-weight materials. For distance vehicles, it is best to make your own wheels from light weight matte board. **In all cases, remove mass to form spoked wheels.**

COMPACT DISK

DREMEL TOOL

## Rotational Inertia

# Making a Wheel from a Compact Disc

**Compact discs** *make excellent wheels for mouse-trap cars, but there is one common problem: fitting the wheel onto an axle. A solution is to use a* **spacer** *that fits into the CD's hole in order to change its size. A* **1/4 L faucet washer** *can be found at a local hardware store and can be used to decrease the size of the hole in a compact disc.*

1/4 L SINK WASHER USED AS A WHEEL SPACER

41

COMPACT DISK

SINK WASHER

BRASS TUBING

**DON'T FORGET to remove mass from the inside of your wheels!**

**Rotational Inertia**

Perhaps the concept most central to building mouse-trap cars is **energy**. Energy is defined as having the ability to do work. Work is motion that result in something being done. Without energy, the universe would be motionless and without life. We usually observe energy only when it is happening or when it is being transformed. Energy can be classified in a number of ways. Most commonly energy is classified as **potential** and **kinetic**. The energy that is stored and held in readiness is called potential energy (PE) because in the stored state it has the potential to do work. For example, a stretched or compressed spring has the potential for doing work. When a bow is drawn, energy is stored in the bow. A stretched rubber band has potential energy because of its position and because in this position it is capable of doing work. Kinetic energy (KE) is energy of motion or the energy a moving object has. A baseball thrown through the air has kinetic energy because of its motion just as a moving car has energy because of its speed or motion.

Energy, potential or kinetic, follows one basic rule called the Law of Conservation of Energy, stated: **Energy cannot be created or destroyed; it may be transformed from one form into another, but the total amount of energy never changes.** By winding the spring on your mouse-trap car, you store energy in the spring as potential energy. This stored potential energy will turn into kinetic energy as the mouse-trap car begins to move. In a perfect universe, your mouse-trap car should roll

POTENTIAL ENERGY (PE)

KINETIC ENERGY (KE)

**42**

TRAP NOT SET

TRAP SET

STORED POTENTIAL ENERGY

forever as the potential energy is changed into kinetic energy. But in our universe there is friction and in order to overcome friction you have to do work. Friction converts energy into **heat** and **sound** which removes energy from your motion, causing the vehicle to roll to a stop as its energy is removed. Your goal in building a good distance car is to produce a vehicle that loses energy at the lowest possible rate.

**43**

KINETIC ENERGY

WAP!

HEAT AND SOUND

# Key Idea

*When building mouse-trap cars, the objective is to transform the stored energy of the spring into* **forward motion**. *By reducing and eliminating friction, your vehicle will be more efficent at converting energy into motion.*

# Kinetic Energy
## Energy of Motion

**Energy**

When designing a mouse-trap powered car, there are two variables that truly determine the overall performance: **friction** and **energy**. Friction is what slows and stops your vehicle; energy is what moves your vehicle. If your vehicle encounters too much friction, your energy supply will be consumed too quickly and your vehicle will not travel very far or accelerate very fast. Evaluate every moving component on your vehicle and decrease the amount of friction at each point. As a general rule of thumb, the more moving components that a machine has, the greater the force of friction will be and the greater the energy consumption will be. **Your ultimate goal when building a distance mouse-trap powered vehicle is to reduce friction to the lowest possible force.** The smaller the frictional force, the farther your supply of energy will propel your vehicle. With this idea in mind, slow-moving vehicles will have a smaller force of air resistance acting against them and will travel farther than faster-moving vehicles.

AIR FRICTION

FRICTION LEVER

BEARING FRICTION

AIR FRICTION

## Energy

FROM
ARM

SPRING
FRICTION

BEARING
FRICTION

## Friction is your Foe

**It can not be said enough!** *Your ultimate goal when building a distance mouse-trap powered vehicle is to reduce friction to the lowest possible force. The smaller the frictional force, the further your supply of energy will propel your vehicle or the faster your vehicle will travel. If you are building a distace car, your vehicle should move as slow as possible without stopping as the spring releases its energy. Look your car over with a scrutinizing eye in order to reduce the total amount of friction acting on your vehicle.*

**Energy**

There is no difference in the amount of energy expended when you walk up a flight of stairs and when you run up a flight of stairs, but there is a difference in the amount of **power** output in the two situations. More power is expended running up the stairs. Power is the rate at which you do work or use energy. Because running up the stairs allows you to get to the top more quickly, you use energy at a higher rate. Higher power ratings mean that more work is being done per second when compared to smaller power ratings. A watt is the unit of measurement for power. A 120 watt light bulb uses twice the energy each second compared to a 60 watt light bulb. Usually higher rates of energy consumption will

60 WATTS

120 WATTS

waste more energy to heat and sound than lower power outputs.

When you build a mouse-trap car for distance, you want a small energy consumption per second or a small power usage. **Smaller power outputs will produce less wasted energy and greater efficiency**. When you build a vehicle for speed, you want to use your energy quickly or at a high power ratio. You can change the power ratio of your vehicle by changing one or all of the following: where the string attaches to the mouse-trap's lever arm, the drive wheel diameter, or the drive axle diameter.

The amount of energy used by a short lever arm and a long lever arm are the same, but the distance that the energy is used determines that rate of energy consumption or the power. Long lever arms decrease the pulling force but increase the pulling distance, thereby decreasing the power. Short lever arms increase the pulling force and decrease the pulling distance, thereby increasing the power. **If you are building a mouse-trap car for speed, you will want the maximum power output** just before the point where the wheels begin to spin-out on the floor. Maximum power output means a higher rate of stored energy is being transferred into energy of motion or greater acceleration of the vehicle. Greater acceleration can be achieved by having a short length lever arm or by having a small axle to a large wheel. **If you are building a distance vehicle, you want to minimize the power output** or transfer stored energy into energy of motion at a slow rate. This usually mean having a long lever arm and a large axle-to-wheel ratio. If you make the lever arm too long, you may not have enough torque through the entire pulling distance to keep the vehicle moving, in which case you will have to attach the string to a lower point or change the axle-to-wheel ratio.

MORE POWER

LESS POWER

47

A GOOD DISTANCE CAR

LONG LEVER ARM

TRAP

COMPACT DISK WHEELS

LARGE AXLE TO WHEEL RATIO

MOTION

**Energy**

# Transmission

The diameters of your drive wheel and drive axle represent your **gearing** or **transmission**. A transmission is any device that transmits mechanical energy from one place to another. With a mouse-trap car, power is transferred to the wheels via the transmission. In addition to getting energy from one place to another, the transmission can be used to trade speed for torque or torque for speed. Some of the common ways to transfer power to the drive wheels are direct drive, gear drive, belt drive, and friction drive. Not all are best used on a mouse-trap car. Gear and pulley ratios are used to describe the mechanical advantage. One gear or pulley is called the "drive" and the other the "driven." The diameter or **ratio** of the drive and driven components of a transmission determines the force and speed that will result. Obviously, there are tradeoffs that

GREATER MECHANICAL ADVANTAGE

MORE POWER

LESS MECHANICAL ADVANTAGE

LESS POWER

you need to understand. When a large gear or pulley is driven by a smaller gear or pulley, there is an increase in torque and a decrease in top speed. When a smaller gear or pulley is driven by a larger gear or pulley, there is a decrease in torque and an increase in top speed. Think of pedaling a multispeed bike. When the rear gear on a bike is as small as possible (i.e., it's in high gear), the bike can go the fastest on a level road, but as the road begins to slant upwards the bike begins to slow. More torque is required to propel the bike up the hill. By putting the bike into a lower gear, you increase the mechanical advantage of your gearing and consequently get more torque, but at the cost of less speed. It is important to match your transmission with the activity you need to perform. A Formula 1 race car and a tractor both have transmissions designed for the tasks they perform. A tractor needs more torque than a race car

IF LARGE GEAR IS THE DRIVER...
- LESS MECHANICAL ADVANTAGE
- MORE SPEED
- LESS TORQUE

IF THE SMALL GEAR IS THE DRIVER...
- GREATER MECHANICAL ADVANTAGE
- LESS SPEED
- MORE TORQUE

**Energy**

but with the tradeoff of speed. Test your mouse-trap car by running the car in your hand. If you place your vehicle on the ground and the mouse-trap lever does not pull off the start or stops part of the way through its motion, you do not have enough torque. If you do not have enough torque you should increase the mechanical advantage by doing one of the following: making the length of the lever arm smaller, using smaller diameter drive wheels, or using a larger diameter drive axle. The larger the diameter of the driven gear or pulley, the greater the mechanical advantage or torque.

MORE FORCE, BUT LESS PULLING DISTANCE

LESS FORCE, BUT MORE PULLING DISTANCE

DIRECT DRIVE

DRIVE WHEEL

AXLE SHAFT ATTACHED DIRECTLY TO DRIVE WHEEL →

FRICTION DRIVE

FRICTION DISK RUBS DIRECTLY ON DRIVE WHEEL

DRIVE WHEEL

GEAR DRIVE

GEARS

DRIVE WHEEL

BELT DRIVE

DRIVE WHEEL →

BELT

PULLEY

PULLEY

**Energy**

By increasing or decreasing the wheel-to-axle ratio, you will change the **mechanical advantage** of your mouse-trap car. Keep in mind, changing the **mechanical advantage does not increase the work you get from your mouse trap; it only changes the size of the force and the distance the force is applied**. With distance vehicles, you want a small force over a long distance; therefore, use a large wheel with a small axle (i.e., a large wheel-to-axle ratio). A large wheel with a small axle will cover more distance per each turn of the axle when compared to a smaller wheel with the same axle. There is a trade-off for having a large wheel-to-axle ratio. The trade-off is that it takes more force to accelerate the vehicle to the same speed in the same time as a vehicle that has a small wheel-to-axle ratio, but this is okay because distance cars should not be fast in order to cut down on air resistance. It is essential that a vehicle with a large wheel-to-axle ratio has a small rotational inertia wheel, since low rotational inertia wheels will be much easier to rotate than large rotational inertia wheels.

For quicker accelerations, a large axle size means a larger force is transferred to the ground, causing greater acceleration. By decreasing the wheel-to-axle ratio, you will increase the torque but at the cost of decreasing the distance that the force is being applied. To achieve quicker accelerations with a speed car, use a wheel or wheels with a large axle or a smaller wheel-to-axle ratio than with your distance car. Again, a tapered axle can be designed to distribute larger forces at the start and then decrease the force once the car is in motion.

LARGE AXLE : WHEEL RATIO

THIN AXLE

**Use a large wheel-to-axle ratio with distance vehicales**

SMALL AXLE : WHEEL RATIO

LARGE AXLE

**Use a small wheel-to-axle ratio with speed vehicles**

50

# Changing the Torque with Axle Size

MASKING TAPE

DRIVE AXLE

If your vehicle does not have enough torque in order to move off the start, it will not travel the full length of the pulling distance without stopping. Try wrapping **tape** around the drive axle in order to increase the **diameter** and increase the **torque**.

## Brain Tip **51**

TAPERED AXLE

TOP VIEW

MORE TORQUE, MORE ACCELERATION

LESS TORQUE, LESS ACCELERATION

It is possible to build a **tapered transmission** that will change the torque throughout the motion of the lever arm's travel distance. If you need more torque off the start and less torque towards the end of travel, start winding the string at the thinner part of the gearing so that it starts to unwind from the thicker diameter at the beginning of its travel. If you need more torque towards the end of the vehicle's motion, start winding the string around the thicker part so that it starts to unwind from the smaller diameter.

# Construction Tip

## Changing an Axle Size

**STEP ONE**

BALL BEARING — AXLE

THE AXLE'S DIAMETER IS TOO BIG FOR THE BEARING

...BUT IT **CAN** BE FIXED!

**STEP TWO**

DRILL

AXLE

PLACE THE AXLE INTO THE DRILL

**STEP THREE**

DRILL

FILE

AXLE

WHILE SPINNING THE AXLE, USE A FILE TO "SHAVE-DOWN" THE AXLE'S DIAMETER

**STEP FOUR**

FILED-DOWN AXLE

BEARING

SLIDE YOUR NEWLY FILED AXLE INTO THE BALL BEARING

PERFECT FIT!

*If you have a hard time finding an axle to fit a bearing or a wheel, **file** or **sand** a larger size axle to fit a smaller hole.*

# Construction Tip

BEARING

GLUE

BEARINGS GLUED DIRECTLY TO THE FRAME **DO NOT** HOLD WELL... IT IS BEST TO MOUNT BEARINGS INTO A BEARING HOLDER OR MAKE A NOTCH IN THE FRAME.

**STEP ONE**

USE AN AXLE WRAPPED IN SAND-PAPER TO FORM NOTCHES FOR BEARINGS

AXLE WRAPPED IN SANDPAPER

**STEP TWO**

SANDED-OUT NOTCH

REMOVE TAPE AND SEPARATE THE TWO SIDE WALLS, AS SHOWN ABOVE

**STEP THREE**

BEARING HOLDER

BEARING

GLUE BEARING HOLDERS IN THE NOTCHES

**STEP FOUR**

AXLE TURNS EASILY

AFTER BEARINGS ARE PLACED INTO THE BEARING HOLDERS, SLIDE THE AXLE INTO PLACE. IT SHOULD SPIN PERFECTLY!

Mounting a Bearing to a Frame

53

# Torque

KNOB IS PLACED TOO CLOSE TO HINGES

When you turn a water faucet, open a door, or tighten a nut with a wrench, you exert a turning force called a **torque**. Torque is the rotational counterpart of **force**. You apply a force to make an object move or accelerate in a particular direction. You apply a torque to make an object turn or rotate. A torque is produced when a force is exerted with **leverage**. For example, a doorknob is on the opposite side of the door from the hinges in order to increase the leverage. By placing the doorknob far from the turning axis of the hinges, less force is required when you push or pull on the doorknob. Less effort is required to use a long wrench than a short wrench to loosen a nut because you have more leverage with a long handle. The distance from the turning axis to the point of contact is called the **lever arm** when the force is applied perpendicularly. Therefore, torque is the product of the lever arm and the force that tends to produce rotation. It is important to note the direction of your applied force. You push or pull the doorknob **perpendicular** to the plane of the door.

**Physics Rules!**

*As the lever arm begins to pull the vehicle, the angle of the pulling force will change with the lever arm until the pulling angle is "zero," at which point the lever arm will fall quickly without any tension in the string.*

TORQUE DECREASES AS ANGLE DECREASES FROM 90°

MAX TORQUE

**Torque**

# String Tension & Torque

The key to a quick start is the proper relationship between the **tension on the string** and the **grip friction of the tires**. If the pulling force on the string is too large, the tires will spin at the start, wasting the spring's energy and thus decreasing performance. The tension of the pulling string should be at its maximum for a speed vehicle but not large enough to cause the wheels to spin off the start. By adjusting the length of the mouse trap's lever arm, you can vary the force that is applied to the wheels of your car. Long lever arms decrease the pulling force while short arms increase the pulling force. **Upon release, energy will be wasted if the arm is not properly positioned. The pulling string must pull perpendicular to the axle's radius for maximum performance at the start!** Lever arms should not extend past the axle when in the lowered position. Reposition the mouse-trap by moving it away from or towards the winding axle if this situation occurs.

TIE STRING ABOVE THE DRIVE AXLE

For distance cars, the tension on the pulling string should be just enough to start the car rolling and maintain a somewhat constant motion throughout its journey. On a distance vehicle, adjust the lever arm to the point where the mouse-trap car almost stops moving. The longer the length of the lever arm that you use, the more string you can wind around the drive axle. Therefore, a greater overall travel distance can occur as the string is pulled off the drive axle. Less pulling force is transferred to the wheels when a long lever arm is used. For this reason, you must reduce the required pulling force by reducing friction and rotational inertia to the absolute minimum, which will always translate into longer lever arms and greater travel distances.

MORE FORCE, BUT LESS PULLING DISTANCE

LESS FORCE, BUT MORE PULLING DISTANCE

## Torque

# Construction Tip
# Trap Placement

MORE FORCE, LESS PULLING DISTANCE

LESS FORCE, MORE PULLING DISTANCE

DEPENDING ON TRAP PLACEMENT, STRING **MUST** BE POSITIONED ON THE LEVER ARM SO THAT IT IS ALIGNED WITH THE DRIVE AXLE POSITION

CORRECT LEVER ARM LENGTH (REACHES AXLE)

INCORRECT LEVER ARM LENGTH (TOO LONG)

A **perpendicular** push or pull provides the greatest amount of rotation for the least amount of effort; for this reason, it is important that the drive axle and lever arm are correctly positioned for the start. When the string is fully wound around the drive axle, the position where the string is tied to the lever arm should be **directly above** the drive axle. At this point the string will be pulled perpendicularly from the lever arm.

**Torque**

# Construction Tip

## Changing the Length of the Lever Arm

**1** LIFT TRAP ARM AND SNIP THE UPPER-LEFT CORNER

*SNAP!*

LEFT CORNER OF TRAP ARM

WIRE CUTTERS

**2** REMOVE LOOSE PIECE OF TRAP ARM

**3** SLIDE ON LONG PIECE OF BRASS TUBING

BRASS TUBING (1/8 IN. DIAMETER)

SPRING FITS OVER TUBING

**4** GLUE

GLUE STRING TO THE END OF THE BRASS TUBING

STRING

*The length of the mouse trap's arm can be extended using a **metal rod**; this will decrease the pulling force from the spring. When replacing the mouse-trap's arm with a longer arm, make sure the replacing arm is strong enough not to bend when under a load. Choose a rigid material that does not bend as easily (e.g., copper or brass rods).*

**Torque**

# Building the Perfect Distance Cars

## Brain Tip

For a good distance car, your design should have the string engaged with the axle for the longest possible period of time by using a long lever arm and having large diameter wheels with a small axle. This will ensure that with each turn of the axle the car travels a greater distance. Your vehicle should have the lowest possible energy consumption; this means that your vehicle should be a slow mover. The larger the drive wheel, the better. Wheels can be as large as 2-3 feet diameter. Decrease mass by building a light frame and by removing mass from the wheels. Test different mouse traps in order to find the one trap the has the greatest tension. The longer the lever arm you can have, the more string you can wind around the drive axle, translating into more travel distance. Using this principle, mouse-trap cars have traveled **100⁺ meters!**

A GOOD DISTANCE CAR

TRAP

COMPACT DISK WHEELS

*At low speeds, **air resistance** is not a large factor in the motion of a moving object, but as the speed of an object increases, the force of air resistance also increases; therefore, at higher speeds moving objects will have to expend more energy to maintain constant velocity.* **For this reason, it is best to build a slow moving distance car!**

**Distance Car**

LONG LEVER ARM

LARGE AXLE TO WHEEL RATIO

MOTION

59

4 INCHES

DISTANCE PULLED BY LEVER ARM

8 INCHES

The **longer** the lever arm, the more string that can be wound around the drive axle and the greater the pulling distance.

LONGER LEVER ARMS PULL VEHICLES FURTHER

**Distance Car**

# Ideas for Increasing Distance

**1** *Decrease rolling friction by re-working the friction points.  Polish bushings or use ball bearings.  If you are using bearings, soak them in WD-40; this will remove any oil or grease.  Although grease and oil are lubricants and often used to reduce friction, adding them to mouse-trap car bearings slows the car down because of the large viscosity of the lubricants.*

## SEE PAGES 6, 9, 13

FRICTION POINTS BETWEEN AXLE AND FRAME

**2** *Decrease the force required to pull the vehicle by decreasing the rotational inertia.   Decrease the rotational inertia by removing mass from the inside of the wheels.  Decrease the overall mass of the car by removing mass from the frame and use  a light-weight lever arm.  Move the trap away from the pulling axle and extend the lever arm.  Re-adjust the string and the string attachment point.*

## SEE PAGES  24, 25, 40, 56

**3** *Use a larger drive wheel.  Try making a wheel out of mat board. Mat board is stiff and light weight.*

## SEE PAGE 17

**Distance Car**

**60**

**4** *Use a smaller drive axle. The larger the ratio of drive wheel(s)-to-axle(s) diameter, the farther you car will go for each turn of the wheel and the greater the pulling distance will be.*

## SEE PAGES 16, 47, 48, 49, 50

LARGE
AXLE:WHEEL
RATIO

THIN
AXLE

**5** *Find a stronger mouse trap. Test different mouse traps in order to find the strongest one.*

**6** *If your car is stopping and the spring is not at its resting point, find a stronger mouse trap or try to make a tapered axle so you can change the torque required to turn the wheels as the pulling force to the drive axle changes, or build up the drive axle with tape.*

## SEE PAGES 48, 49, 50, 51

MASKING
TAPE

DRIVE
AXLE

TAPERED
AXLE

**7** *Check string alignment and make sure that the string is attached directly over the drive axle with the lever arm held in the fully wound position.*

## SEE PAGES 55, 56

**Distance Car**

# Building the Perfect Speed Cars

## Brain Tip

Wheels should be around 2-5 inches in diameter or no larger than a compact disc. Use large diameter axles or build the axles up with tape. The vehicle should be designed to have a large energy consumption in a short period of time (i.e., a large power output). Build a car that gets up to top speed as quick as possible (i.e., in the shortest distance). Use rubber bands on the drive wheels and/or Traction Action® on the wheels in order to increase the traction. More traction means greater acceleration. The vehicles frame should be short and light weight. Your vehicle should have a small wheel-to-axle ratio and a short lever arm. If the lever arm is too short or the wheel-to-axle ratio is too small, your vehicle will slip off the start and will waste energy. Therefore, adjust either variable in order to find the best performance.

PLACE A LOOP IN THE STRING AND MAKE SURE THE LENGTH OF THE STRING JUST REACHES THE AXLE HOOK (2 LEVER-ARM LENGTHS)

MASKING TAPE

DRIVE AXLE

SMALL AXLE: WHEEL RATIO

LARGE AXLE

**Speed Car**

*By wrapping tape around the drive axle you can decrease the wheel-to-axle ratio and increase the power.*

IF WHEELS ARE SPINNING ON THE START MOVE THE MOUSE TRAP **AWAY** FROM THE DRIVE AXLE AND EXTEND THE LEVER ARM

MORE POWER

LESS POWER

63

*Use the shortest possible lever arm. This will start the vehicle without spinning the tires.*

**Speed Car**

## 1
*Move the mouse trap closer to the drive axle as long as the wheels are not spinning and decrease lever arm accordingly.*

**SEE PAGES 24, 37, 55, 56**

MORE SPEED

FRONT AXLE

## 2
*Increase traction on drive wheels by using rubber bands or the middle section of a rubber balloon around the drive wheels. Try adding mass directly above the drive axle.*

**SEE PAGES 18, 19, 37, 38**

RUBBER BAND

## 3
*Move the trap away from drive wheel(s)* **only if the wheels are slipping**. *This will decrease the pulling force which is the reason for the slipping wheels.*

**SEE PAGES 37, 38, 56**

**Speed Car**

**4** *Decrease rolling friction by re-working the friction points. Polish bushings or use ball bearings. If you are using bearings, soak them in WD-40l; this will remove any oil or grease. Although grease and oil are lubricants and often used to reduce friction, adding them to mouse-trap car bearings slows the car down because of the large viscosity of the lubricants.*

## SEE PAGES 6, 9, 13

FRICTION POINTS BETWEEN AXLE AND FRAME

SPIN A BEARING ON A PENCIL TO REMOVE GREASE AFTER SOAKING IN ALCOHOL

**5** *Decrease rotational inertia of wheels by removing mass from the inside of the wheels. Also, try smaller diameter wheels.*

## SEE PAGES 25, 40

**6** *Decrease the wheel-to-axle ratio by adding tape to the drive axle.*

## SEE PAGES 50, 51

SMALL AXLE: WHEEL RATIO

LARGE AXLE

MASKING TAPE

DRIVE AXLE

**7** *Check string alignment and make sure that the string is attached directly over the drive axle with the lever arm held in the fully wound position.*

## SEE PAGES 55, 56

**Speed Car**

## PROBLEM:

*Axle slides back and forth causing wheels to rub against the frame of the car, slowing or stopping the car.*

1. Add thrust washer between wheels and the frame for a smoother rubbing surface with less friction.

THRUST WASHER

2. Make spacers out of brass tubing to hold the wheels in place and limit the side-to-side play of the wheels or axles.

3. If you are using bearings, the axle may be moving side to side. Carefully glue the axles to the bearings without getting glue in the bearings.

BEARING

AXLE

GLUE

## PROBLEM:

*Can't find an axle to fit the wheels or bearings.*

1. Re-size the axle or change the wheel's hole size with a spacer.

¼ L SINK WASHER USED AS A WHEEL SPACER

## PROBLEM:

*Mouse trap falls quickly but car moves slowly.*

   **1.** Drive wheels are not glued to the axle
      and the axle is spinning inside the
      wheels. Glue wheels to axle.

   **2.** There is no hook on the axle for attaching
      the string and/or the string is slipping off the axle without pulling.
      The hook may not be glued to the axle and is slipping under the tension
      of the string.

## PROBLEM:

*Mouse trap car does not start or moves slowly.*

   **1.** Too much friction in the rolling points. Re-do the rolling points or
      try ball bearings.

## Technical Help

## PROBLEM:

*Mouse trap car does not start or moves slowly. (Continued)*

> **2.** Not enough tension in the pulling string. Move the trap closer to the drive axle and adjust the string attachment point on the lever arm accordingly *or* try to build up the drive axle with tape. Lastly, test different mouse traps and use the strongest one.

## PROBLEM:

*Mouse trap car does not travel straight.*

> **1.** Wheels are not pointing in the same direction. The solution is to bring the wheels into alignment. If the vehicle is a three-wheeled vehicle you need to focus your efforts on the single wheel. Try to align it with the other two. This is not easy!

> **2.** This only applies to long distance cars that use one large wheel as the drive wheel. If the car travels straight when you push it without the tension of the lever arm, but turns once under the pulling tension of the trap, there is too much frame flex or the trap is pulling too hard on one side of the axle. Strengthen the frame or prevent the pulling side of the axle from giving too much at its holding points.

## Technical Help

## PROBLEM:

*Mouse-trap car suddenly stops or slows quickly.*

1. The string is not releasing from the drive axle because it is either glued to the axle or it is too long *or* the hook is too long and caching the string causing it to rewind.

*Cut string a little bit* **shorter** *than what is needed in order to insure a proper release.*

2. There is too much friction at the rolling points. Re-work the bearings to reduce friction or try ball bearings.

FRICTION POINTS BETWEEN AXLE AND FRAME

ROLLER BALLS

BALL BEARING

3. Wheels are rubbing on the frame. Prevent wheels from rubbing with spacers or thrust washers.

THRUST WASHER

**Technical Help**

A = 1 x Wood Sheet (1/4" x 3" x 18" )
B = 1 x Wood Sheet (1/4" x 3" x 12" )
C = 4 x CD Wheels
E = 8 x Sink Washers (1/4 L)
F = 4 x #10 SAE Flat Washers
G = 24" of Kevlar String

H = 1 x Mouse Trap
I = Several Rubber Bands
J = Twist Tie for axle hook
K = Brass Axle (2) (1/8" dia. x 12")
L = Brass Axle (3/16" dia. x 12")

**The wood sheets are cut from one 36" x 3" x 1/4" Balsa Wood strip**

## Brain Tip

By **taping** the side rails together before you do any drilling or marking, you can insure that the axle holes and top deck markings will line up.

## WARNING!

Cut only with a sharp razor. Make small little scoring cuts until you cut through the wood. Use only a metal-edged ruler as a guide!

TAKE THE 18" PIECE AND USE AN EXACTO KNIFE TO **SCORE** IT DOWN THE MIDDLE WITH A METAL RULER AS YOUR GUIDE. MAKE SURE IT SPLITS EVENLY.

18"

12"

METAL RULER

7/32" DRILL BIT

TAPE RAILS TOGETHER AND MARK THEM FOR DECK PLACEMENT. DRILL TWO HOLES USING A 7/32" DRILL BIT.

TAKE A 36" INCH PIECE OF LIGHT WOOD AND CUT IT INTO 12", 18", AND 6" PIECES, AS SHOWN.

18"

6"

12"

DISCARD

DISCARD THE 6" PIECE. MAKE SURE THAT YOUR CUTS ARE CLEAN AND SANDED SO AS TO REDUCE AIR FRICTION. THE 12" PIECE WILL BECOME THE "DECK TOP" AND THE 18" PIECE WILL BECOME THE "SIDE RAILS."

## Brain Tip

*I discovered this tip one day in the labotory by accident:* **White glue** *is by far the best glue to use because it soaks into wood and dries flexibly. The down side to using white glue is the long drying time. Here's a time-saver! Apply white glue to what you are gluing and have a friend squirt some super glue onto the white glue as you hold your pieces together. The super glue causes the white glue to harden quickly, saving time.*

72

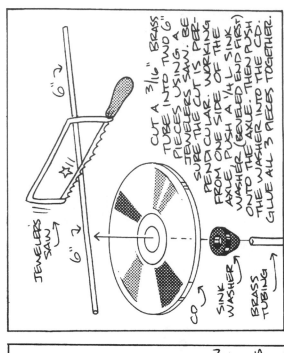

CUT A 3/16" BRASS TUBE INTO TWO 6" PIECES USING A JEWELERS SAW. BE SURE THE CUT IS PERPENDICULAR. WORKING FROM ONE SIDE OF THE AXLE, PUSH A 1/4L SINK WASHER (BEVELED END FIRST) ONTO THE AXLE. THEN PUSH THE WASHER INTO THE CD. GLUE ALL 3 PIECES TOGETHER.

JEWELERS SAW →

6"?

6"?

CD ↗

SINK WASHER ↗

BRASS TUBING ↗

MAKE SURE YOU ALIGN THE SIDE RAILS SO THAT THE AXLE HOLES LINE UP.

GLUE DECK ONTO SIDE RAILS USING THE MARKINGS AS A GUIDE. ELMER'S WHITE GLUE IS RECOMMENDED ANY TIME YOU ARE GLUING WOOD TOGETHER.

GLUE

REMOVE LOOSE PIECE OF TRAP ARM. SAVE THIS PIECE FOR THE NEXT STEP.

LIFT TRAP ARM AND SNIP THE UPPER LEFT CORNER, AS SHOWN.

WIRE CUTTERS

LEFT CORNER OF TRAP ARM

NEXT, SLIDE ANOTHER SINK WASHER (OPPOSITE ORIENTATION) DOWN THE AXLE FOLLOWED BY A #10 FLAT WASHER, AS SHOWN. SLIDE THE AXLE INTO THE FRAME AND REPEAT REVERSING THE LAST TWO STEPS; ADDING THE FLAT WASHER, SINK WASHER, THEN GLUING ON THE OTHER SINK WASHER, AND CD.

DO NOT GLUE

CD

SINK WASHERS

FLAT WASHER

#10 FLAT WASHER

SINK WASHER

## Brain Tip

*Glue rubber bands around the edge of your drive wheels if you are building a speed car. This will increase the traction between the tires and the floor causing greater acceleration*

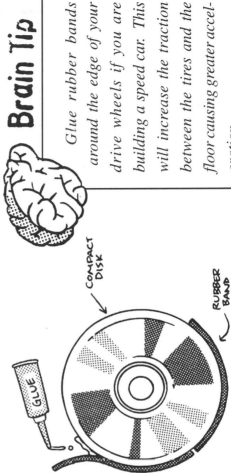

COMPACT DISK

RUBBER BAND

GLUE

*Do not forget to remove mass from the wheels for increased performance. Also, if you are building a speed car, add **rubber bands** to the edge of the wheels.*

**74**

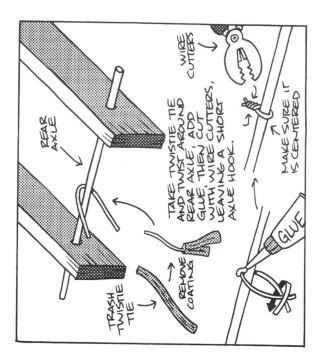

REAR AXLE

TRASH TWISTIE TIE

REMOVE COATING

WIRE CUTTERS

TAKE TWISTIE TIE AND TWIST AROUND REAR AXLE, ADD GLUE, THEN CUT WITH WIRE CUTTERS, LEAVING A SHORT AXLE HOOK.

MAKE SURE IT IS CENTERED

GLUE

LEVER ARM SHOULD REACH REAR AXLE

MORE SPEED

MORE PULLING DISTANCE

CHOOSE WHERE YOU WANT TO PLACE YOUR LEVER ARM; CLOSE TO THE REAR AXLE FOR MORE SPEED OR FARTHER AWAY FOR MORE PULLING DISTANCE.

SLIDE 1/8"D BRASS TUBE ONTO THE TRAP ARM

SPRING FITS OVER TUBING

SNIP END OF DISCARDED TRAP ARM AND SLIDE INTO THE OTHER END OF THE TUBE. ADD GLUE.

DISCARDED TRAP ARM

END OF LEVER ARM

*Make sure that you trim the hook so that it does not snag, causing the string to re-wind around the axle.*

LEVER ARM

SLIDE THE LONG PIECE OF BRASS TUBING ONTO THE ATTACHED TRAP ARM UNDER THE SPRING.

CHOOSE WHERE YOU WANT TO PLACE YOUR LEVER ARM: **CLOSE** TO THE DRIVE AXLE FOR MORE SPEED OR **FARTHER AWAY** FOR MORE PULLING DISTANCE. CUT THE LEVER ARM SO THAT IT REACHES THE DRIVE AXLE.

MORE PULLING DISTANCE

MORE SPEED

FRONT AXLE

STRING SHOULD REACH REAR AXLE EXACTLY.

NOW THAT YOU HAVE FINISHED YOUR CAR, GO BACK AND MAKE ANY NEEDED, SMALL ADJUSTMENTS TO IMPROVE PERFORMANCE. MAKE SURE THE AXLES SPIN SMOOTHLY, AND ADJUST THE LOOSE WASHERS TO FIT. THE STRING AND LEVER ARM SHOULD REACH THE AXLE HOOK. YOU SHOULD NOT EXPECT YOUR CAR TO WORK THE FIRST TIME. **YOU WILL HAVE TO MAKE ADJUSTMENTS!** GOOD LUCK!

STRING (KEVLAR™ IS RECOMMENDED)

FOLD A SMALL PART OF THE STRING OVER ITSELF TO FORM A LOOP

HOLD THE ENDS TOGETHER AND PULL THROUGH, AS SHOWN.

AFTER THE LOOP IS THROUGH, PULL UNTIL A KNOT IS FORMED

PULL TIGHT

KNOT

MEASURE DISTANCE BETWEEN LEVER ARM AND REAR AXLE. CUT STRING SAME LENGTH.

GLUE OTHER END TO LEVER ARM

75

The Finished Product
Lets Go Racing!

Good Luck

76

# Notes for The Teacher

Mousetrap car competitions have been a favorite activitie of mine and my students from the first year I introduced it in 1991. The first year the distance record was set at 12 meters. Today the current record at McNeil High School is 111 meters. Only through a complete understanding of the physics behind mousetrap cars have we been able to achieve such great performance. This is a collection of lab activities that I (Doc Fizzix) have designed in order to help my students fully see how the different variables affect the performance of both speed and distance mousetrap-powered vehicles. Students have to know the variables in order to push their creations to the outer limits. Mousetrap cars are machines and all machines have to be in balance with their surroundings in order to work efficiently. Over exaggeration of one or more variables can lead to poor performance and disaster. By performing the following activities students can find a harmonious balance that will produce the best results for their vehicles.

It may be necessary for you to modify various parts of the different lab activities in order to meet your teaching needs or goals. My method for testing a variable may not be the best possible method, but the overall process through which the lab was designed is more important in my classroom. No activities can be successful unless the teacher participates in the different activities with the students. The teacher must take time to discuss various results with the class as individuals and/or groups discover them.

LEVER ARM

STRING

PULLING FORCE

STRING WRAPPED AROUND DRIVE AXLE

MOTION

# Lab #1- Chasing the Mouse

## Purpose

To analyze the motion of a mousetrap powered vehicle over 5 meters.

## Equipment Needed

Ticker Timer
Ticker Tape
Meter Stick
Stopwatch

## Discussion

In this experiment you will collect data from your mousetrap car using a ticker timer. A ticker timer is a device that makes marks on a ticker tape at equal intervals of time. A long piece of ticker tape will be attached to the back of your mousetrap vehicle. As your vehicle is in motion the ticker timer will leave a series of marks on the tape that is attached to your vehicle. Because the time between each mark is the same, a variety of variables can be measured and calculated from the position of each mark. I recommend analyzing the motion of your car over a five meter distance. After your vehicle has made its run, you will be measuring the distance from the first mark to each of the following marks. Velocity is the rate at which your vehicle is covering distance. The greater the rate, the more distance that is being covered per time. The average velocity is the travel distance divided by the travel time. The actual velocity at each mark is calculated from the average velocity by using Formula #2 from the list of formulas. Acceleration is the rate at which your vehicle is changing velocity. In order to find the acceleration you will have to first find the change in velocity between each point using Formula #3. By dividing the change in velocity for each interval, you will calculate the acceleration between each mark (Formula #4).

# Formulas

**Formula #1:** $\quad \bar{v} = \dfrac{\Delta d}{\Delta t} \qquad \bar{v} = \dfrac{d_{t_f} - d_{t_0}}{\Delta t}$

**Formula #2:** $\quad \bar{a} = \dfrac{\Delta v}{\Delta t} \qquad \bar{a} = \dfrac{v_{t_f} - v_{t_0}}{\Delta t}$

## Using a Stopwatch: Alternative Approach

I suggest timing the vehicle over 5 meters if you plan on using a ticker timer, but if you have a long-distance car that travels great distances, you should not use the ticker timer because the vehicle will become too heavy by pulling of the long ticker tape. You can collect data with an alternative approach: Mark out the floor with masking tape every meter or two meters, depending on the distance that your car will go.

Using a stopwatch that can handle split times, walk along side your mousetrap car and call out the time at each mark on the floor. A partner should be recording the times as you relay them using the split-time function. Calculations are the same, but realize that in this example the distance was held constant and not the time.

**Motion**

*Please take note: It is assumed that the experimenter uses standard S.I. units for all activities.*

# The Set-up

CARBON PAPER

TAPE TIMER

40 ↑ 10
OFF

TAPE THE
TICKER TAPE
TO THE BACK
OF THE CAR
AND INSERT
IT INTO THE
TAPE TIMER
AS SHOWN →

ROLL
OF
TICKER
TAPE

Label one end of the tape as the front. Thread the ticker tape through the timer and attach the front of the tape to the rear of the car using a small piece of tape. Position the tape such that the tape does not get tangled with your vehicle's operations during the timing.

**Motion**

## Ticking Away the Time

**Step 1:** Determine the distance for which the data will be collected. Tear off enough ticker tape to cover the distance of the timing.

**Step 2:** Select or determine the frequency of the ticker timer. The frequency of the ticker tape determines the time between each mark. If the frequency is 10Hz, the time between marks is 0.1s. If the frequency is 60Hz, the time between marks is 1/60 s. Record this frequency in your data table under "time."

**Step 3:** Label one end of the tape as the front. Thread the ticker tape through the timer and attach the front of the tape to the rear of the car using a small piece of tape. Position the tape such that the tape does not get tangled with your vehicle's operations during the timing.

**Step 4:** Place your vehicle at the start line. Line up the ticker timer directly behind the vehicle tape. Straighten the ticker tape behind the timer so that is passes through the timer without binding. Turn the ticker timer on and then release the vehicle. Remove the tape from the vehicle after the run.

## Motion

EACH DOT GETS FURTHER AND FURTHER APART, SHOW- ING ACCELERATION OF THE CAR, SO a EQUALS CHANGE IN VELOCITY OVER TIME...

... OR $a = \frac{\Delta v}{t}$ !

**Step 5:** From the front of the ticker tape, darken each mark and label as follows: $t_0$, $t_1$, $t_2$, $t_3$, $t_4$, $t_5$, ...$t_n$.

**Step 6:** Design a data table where you can record the following: total time (t), distance between marks ($\Delta$d), total distance (d), velocity at mark ($v_f$), change in speed from previous mark ($\Delta$v), acceleration between marks (a).

## Data Table #1

| Total Time | Change in Time | Change in Distance | Total Distance | Change in Velocity | Acceleration |
|---|---|---|---|---|---|
| $t_1=$ | $t_{0,1}=$ | $\Delta d_{0,1}=$ | $d_1=$ | $v_{0,1}=$ | $a_{0,1}=$ |
| $t_2=$ | $t_{1,2}=$ | $\Delta d_{1,2}=$ | $d_2=$ | $v_{1,2}=$ | $a_{1,2}=$ |
| $t_3=$ | $t_{2,3}=$ | $\Delta d_{2,3}=$ | $d_3=$ | $v_{2,3}=$ | $a_{2,3}=$ |

**Step 7:** Measure the distance from the first mark ($t_0$) to the second mark ($t_1$) and record this as ($t_{0,1}$) distance between marks ($\Delta d_{0,1}$). Measure the distance from the second point to the third mark and record this as $t_2$ distance between marks ($\Delta d_{1,2}$). Measure the distance between each of the following marks and record as the distance between marks ($\Delta d_{2,3}$, $\Delta d_{3,4}$, $\Delta d_{4,5}$ ...$\Delta d_n$).

**Step 8:** Add the change in distance between $d_{0,1}$ and record as $d_1$ total distance. Add the change in distance between $d_{0,1}$ and

### Recommendations
*Try to set-up a **spread sheet** on a computer in order to handle your data more **efficiently**.*

**Motion**

$d_{1,2}$ and record as $d_2$ total distance. Add the total distance between $d_{1,2}$ and $d_{2,3}$ and record as $d_3$ total distance. Continue this approach until you have the total distance from each mark to the first point.

**Step 9:** From equation #1 find the average change in velocity between each point or mark on your ticker tape using the following equation:

$$\bar{v} = \frac{\Delta d}{\Delta t}$$

$$\bar{v}_{0,1} = \frac{\Delta d_{0,1}}{\Delta t_{0,1}} \quad , \quad \bar{v}_{1,2} = \frac{\Delta d_{1,2}}{\Delta t_{1,2}} \quad , \quad \bar{v}_{2,3} = \frac{\Delta d_{2,3}}{\Delta t_{2,3}}$$

Record as change in velocity at mark $v_{0,1}$, $v_{1,2}$, $v_{2,3}$, ...$v_n$.

**Step 10:** Calculate the acceleration using formula #2 and record as follows:

$$\bar{a} = \frac{\Delta v}{\Delta t} \quad , \quad a_{01,} = \frac{\bar{v}_1 - \bar{v}_0}{\Delta t_{0,1}}$$

$$a_{1,2} = \frac{\bar{v}_2 - \bar{v}_1}{\Delta t_{1,2}} \quad , \quad a_{2,3} = \frac{\bar{v}_3 - \bar{v}_2}{\Delta t_{2,3}}$$

Record as acceleration between marks as $a_{0,1}$, $a_{1,2}$, $a_{2,3}$, ...$a_n$.

**Motion**

THESE DOTS ARE EVENLY SPACED, SHOWING A CONSTANT VELOCITY, WHERE V EQUALS DISTANCE DIVIDED BY TIME, OR V = D/t !!

# Graphing the results

You will now graph your data in order to learn from your results. In each of the following graphs attempt to draw a "best fit" line. If data is widely scattered do not attempt to connect each dot but instead draw the best line you can that represents the shape of the dots. If you have access to a computer you can use a spread sheet like Microsoft Exel to plot your data.

1. Graph **Total Distance** on the vertical axis and **Total Time** on the horizontal.

2. Graph **Velocity Final** at each point on the vertical axis and **Total Time** on the horizontal.

3. Graph **Acceleration** on the vertical axis and **Total Time** on the horizontal.

# Analysis

1. Identify the time intervals where your vehicle had the maximum positive and negative acceleration. Where did your vehicle have the most constant acceleration?

2. What was the vehicle's maximum speed over the timing distance and at what point did this occur?

3. How far was your vehicle pulled by the string? From the graph is it possible to determine when the string was no longer pulling the vehicle? Explain.

4. Compare your performance to the performance of other vehicles in the class and discuss how yours relates.

# Lab #2 - All Wound Up

## Purpose

To calculate the starting potential energy and to find the spring coefficient.

## Equipment Needed

Spring Scale or a Computer Force Probe
Tension Wheel (recommended but not needed)
String

## Discussion

Energy has the ability to do work. Your mousetrap car's performance will depend directly on the strength of your mousetrap's spring. The stored energy of your spring in the fully wound-up position is called potential energy. The amount of stored potential energy is the same as the work that was required to wind the spring. The force required to wind the spring times the distance the force was applied is equal to the work that was done on the spring (Formula #1). Because the force required to wind the spring changes and depends on how much the spring is wound, you will have to find the average force between a series of points and then calculate the work done between those marks. The total work (or the stored potential energy) is equal to all the changes of energy between all the points added together (Formula #2). In order to measure the winding force you have to use a spring scale attached to a lever. The lever is lifted and the force is measured every 5 or 10 degrees. The scale has to be held such that the string attached to the lever arm is perpendicular. A problem with this method is that as the spring scale is held in different positions it becomes inaccurate. The spring scale cannot change from the position at which it was zeroed. For this reason I recommend using a tension wheel. A tension wheel allows the spring scale to remain in one position, producing more accurate results and it is easier to use.
The distance that the average force was applied is equal to the angle of the

**Potential Energy, Spring Constant**

# The Set-up

PROTRACTOR

TRAP

SPRING SCALE

HOLDING THE PRO-
TRACTOR PARALLEL TO
THE MOUSETRAP, PULL
THE LEVER ARM USING
THE ATTACHED SPRING
SCALE. RECORD THE
TENSION OF THE STRING
AT EACH ANGLE.

measurement in radians
times the length of the measuring lever
arm. If you are using a tension wheel, then the radius of the wheel is
the measuring lever arm (Formula #3). Formula #4 allows you to convert
from degrees to radians.

For a spring that is stretched or compressed longitudinally, Hooke's Law
applies and says that the force is equal to the spring constant times the
stretching or compressing displacement. But a mousetrap spring does not
stretch longitudinally. A mousetrap spring is a torsion spring and winds up.
For this type of spring a different formula is needed (Formula #5). It is a
torque that must be applied to the spring to wind it and the displacement is
measured in radians (Formula #6). The units associated with the spring
constant become Newtons * Meters/ Radians. For a spring that compresses
or stretches in a linear direction, the total potential energy is one half the
spring constant times the displacement squared (Formula #7). For a torsion
spring the displacement is substituted by the angle in radians (Formula #8).

## Potential Energy, Spring Constant

# Tools of the Trade: Tension Wheel

A **tension wheel** is designed to direct the pulling force in the same direction as the spring is wound. This prevents the scale from having to be re-zeroed as its direction of pull changes. Degree markings make it easy to measure force and angle.

EACH DASH REPRESENTS A DEGREE, OR ANGLE. USING THIS TECHNIQUE, YOU CAN FIND THE TENSION OF YOUR STRING AT EACH ANGLE

SPRING SCALE

## How it Works:

As the wheel is turned clockwise the spring on the mousetrap is compressed. The value of the spring constant depends on the material the spring is made from, the diameter of the wire, the diameter of the coil, and the number of coils.

## Need A Tool?

This tool can be ordered from Doc Fizzix at (512) 218-0454
www.docfizzix.com

# Formulas

**Formula #1:** $\quad W = F \cdot d$

Work formula used with a constant (non-changing) force

**Formula #2:** $\quad W = \int_0^{\pi r} F(x)\, d(x)$

Work formula used with a changing force as
with a mousetrap spring

**Formula #3:** $\quad d = \theta r$

A formula to calculate the linear distance of travel for a wheel

**Formula #4:** $\quad \text{degrees} \times \dfrac{\pi}{180^o} = \theta$

A formula used to change degrees into radians

**Formula #5:** $\quad F = -kx$

Hooke's Law. Force of a stretched or compressed spring

**Formula #6:** $\quad \tau = \kappa\theta$

From Hooke's Law. Used to calculate the torque from a torsional spring

**Formula #7:** $\quad PE = \dfrac{1}{2}kx^2$

Potential energy of a stretched or compressed spring

**Formula #8:** $\quad PE = \dfrac{1}{2}\kappa\theta^2$

Potential energy of a stretched or compressed torsion spring

## Potential Energy, Spring Constant

# Pulling Your Weight

PROTRACTOR

TRAP

SPRING SCALE

HOLDING THE PRO-TRACTOR PARALLEL TO THE MOUSETRAP, PULL THE LEVER ARM USING THE ATTACHED SPRING SCALE. RECORD THE TENSION OF THE STRING AT EACH ANGLE.

**Step 1:** In this lab you can use either a spring scale or a force probe in order to measure the spring's tension at different points along its travel. Start by attaching a string to the end of your mousetrap's extended lever arm. The point where you attach the string on the mousetrap's lever arm must extend pass the edge of the mousetrap's base so that all measurements can be taken from 0 to 180 degrees without the mousetrap's base blocking the measuring process. The string should be about 20 centimeters in length or less. Attach the spring scale to the other end of the string. Hold or attach a protractor to the mousetrap so that the center point of the protractor is in the middle of the spring and the zero degree point on the protractor is lined up with the starting point of the relaxed lever arm.

**Step 2:** Start at "0" degrees and pull up on the lever arm with the spring scale until the lever arm "just" lifts up from the base of the mousetrap and record this measurement as the starting force. Continue to pull up on the spring scale, stopping at every 5 or 10 degrees. Record the tension at each point in the data table. You must keep the scale perpendicular to the lever arm at each point you measure. Record the tension and angle in the data table.

## Potential Energy, Spring Constant

# Data Tables

**Recommendations:**
*Try to set-up a* **spread sheet** *on a computer in order to handle your data more* **efficiently**.

## Data Table #1

| Angle | Tension | Change in Radians | Total Radians | Change in Displacement | Total Displacement |
|-------|---------|-------------------|---------------|------------------------|--------------------|
| 5 | $F_0=$ | $\Delta\theta_0=0$ | $\theta_0=0$ | $\Delta d_0=0$ | $d_0=0$ |
| 10 | $F_1=$ | $\Delta\theta_1=$ | $\theta_1=$ | $\Delta d_1=$ | $d_1=$ |
| 15 | $F_2=$ | $\Delta\theta_2=$ | $\theta_2=$ | $\Delta d_2=$ | $d_2=$ |
| 20 | $F_3=$ | $\Delta\theta_3=$ | $\theta_3=$ | $\Delta d_3=$ | $d_3=$ |
| 25 | $F_4=$ | $\Delta\theta_4=$ | $\theta_4=$ | $\Delta d_4=$ | $d_4=$ |
| 180 | $F_{36}=$ | $\Delta\theta_{36}=$ | $\theta_{36}=$ | $\Delta d_{36}=$ | $d_{36}=$ |

## Data Table #2

| Spring Constant | Torque | Change in Potential Energy | Total Potential Energy |
|-----------------|--------|----------------------------|------------------------|
| $k_0=0$ | $T_0=$ | $\Delta PE_0=0$ | $PE_0=0$ |
| $k_1=$ | $T_1=$ | $\Delta PE_1=$ | $PE_{0-1}=$ |
| $k_2=$ | $T_2=$ | $\Delta PE_2=$ | $PE_{0-2}=$ |
| $k_3=$ | $T_3=$ | $\Delta PE_3=$ | $PE_{0-3}=$ |
| $k_4=$ | $T_4=$ | $\Delta PE_4=$ | $PE_{0-4}=$ |
| $k_{36}=$ | $T_{36}=$ | $\Delta PE_{36}=$ | $PE_{0-36}=$ |
| Ave | | Total | |

**Potential Energy, Spring Constant**

**Step 3:** Calculate the change in radians for each angle and record them in the data table. If each measurement was made at the same increment (e.g., 5, 10, 15, 20 …) you can use the same change in radians for all angles. Use the following method to calculate the change in radians:

$$\Delta\theta_1 = (\text{degrees}_1 - \text{degrees}_0) \times \frac{\pi}{180^o}$$

$$\Delta\theta_2 = (\text{degrees}_2 - \text{degrees}_1) \times \frac{\pi}{180^o}$$

**Step 4:** Measure the length of the lever arm from the spring to the point where the scale was attached to the arm and record this as the radius. Calculate the change in displacement, also known as the arc length, for each angle using the following formula. If each measurement was made at the same increment, (e.g. 5, 10, 15, 20 …) you can use the same arc length (displacement) for all angles.

$$\Delta d_1 = \Delta\theta_1 r \qquad\qquad \Delta d_2 = \Delta\theta_2 r \qquad\qquad \Delta d_3 = \Delta\theta_3 r$$

**Step 5:** Calculate the total displacement for each angle by adding each of the previous changes in displacement to the next.

**Step 6:** Calculate the change in potential energy for each point using the following method. Multiply the average force between the starting and ending points with the change in distance. Add each of the change in PE values together in order to find the total potential energy from the column. This added value should be the energy your vehicle starts with before it is released.

**Potential Energy, Spring Constant**

94

$$\Delta PE_{0,1} = \frac{F_0 + F_1}{2} \cdot \Delta d_1$$

$$\Delta PE_{1,2} = \frac{F_1 + F_2}{2} \cdot \Delta d_2$$

$$\Delta PE_{2,3} = \frac{F_2 + F_3}{2} \cdot \Delta d_3$$

**Step 7:** Calculate the spring constant for each change in angle. The spring on a mousetrap is an example of a torsion spring, a spring that coils as opposed to one that stretches; use the following equation to calculate the spring constant: $\tau = \kappa\theta$. Torque is equal to the spring constant times the angle measured in radians. Torque is calculated from the force that is applied to a lever arm times the length of the lever arm. $\tau = Fr_{\text{lever arm}}$ You will need to subtract the starting torque in order to find the actual change in torque for each change in angle. Total each spring constant and find an average.

$$\kappa = \frac{\tau}{\theta}$$

$$\kappa_1 = \frac{(F_1 - F_0)r_{\text{arm length}}}{\theta_{0,1}}$$

$$\kappa_2 = \frac{(F_2 - F_1)r_{\text{arm length}}}{\theta_{1,2}}$$

$$\kappa_3 = \frac{(F_3 - F_2)r_{\text{arm length}}}{\theta_{2,3}}$$

**Potential Energy, Spring Constant**

# Graphing the results

In each of the following graphs attempt to draw the best fit lines. If data is widely scattered do not attempt to connect each dot but instead draw the best shape of the dots. If you have access to a computer, you can use a spread sheet like Microsoft Exel to plot your data.

1. Graph **Pulling Force** on the vertical axis and the **Displacement** on the horizontal axis.

2. Graph **Torque** on the vertical axis and **Angle in Radians** on the horizontal.

GRAPHING THE TENSION AT EACH ANGLE, YOU CAN GET THE **SPRING CONSTANT** AND THE **STARTING ENERGY**. YOUR RESULTS SHOULD ROUGHLY FORM A STRAIGHT LINE.

## Potential Energy, Spring Constant

# Analysis

1. The slope from your graph of "torque vs. angle" represents the spring constant. Does the slope change or remain constant? Do you have an ideal spring that follows Hooke's Law?

2. What does the slope of the line from each of your graphs tell you about the strength of your spring compared to other students' graphs?

3. Calculate the area under all parts of the best-fit line from the graph of "torque vs. angle." This number represents the potential energy you are starting with. The larger the number, the more energy you have to do work. This number should be close to the total potential energy calculated from your data table. How does the slope compare to the number in the data table?

4. How does your potential energy compare to other students' potential energy in your class? Discuss.

# Lab #3 - How Far Can I Go?

## Purpose

To determine the pulling distance, the power output, and the mechanical advantage.

## Equipment Needed

Ruler (A caliper makes smaller measurements easier)
Stopwatch
Meter Tape

## Variables Needed From Other Labs

Total Potential Energy from Lab #2

## Discussion

The pulling distance is the measurement from where the vehicle starts to where the pulling force on the drive axle ends. In this lab you will calculate how far your mousetrap car should be pulled by the mousetrap's lever arm. Once you have predicted the pulling distance you will then measure and time the actual pulling distance in order to find the power rating. The pulling distance does not tell you how far your mousetrap car will travel, only how far it will be pulled by the mousetrap's lever arm. The distance that your mousetrap car is pulled is directly proportional to the size of the drive wheels and the length of string that is wrapped around the drive axle. The travel distance is inversely proportional to the size of the drive axle. What all this means is the following: the larger the drive wheel(s), the greater the pulling distance. The more string that can be pulled off the drive axle, the greater the pulling distance. The larger the drive axle, the shorter the pulling distance. In order to get more string wound around the drive axle, you can do one of the following: use a smaller diameter drive axle or extend the length of the mousetrap's lever arm and then place the trap further from the drive axle.

**Power Output, Gear Ratio, Mechanical Advantage**

The pulling distance is calculated from the number of turns that your wheel makes times the circumference of your wheel. The number of turns that your wheel will make depends on the length of string wound around the pulling axle divided by the circumference of the drive axle. By putting the first two formulas together you can predict the pulling distance.

## Power Output

Power is the rate at which work is being done. Your mousetrap car will convert stored potential energy from the wound-up spring into work to overcome friction. The rate at which your mousetrap car converts this stored energy into work is your vehicles power rating. You will calculate the power rating by dividing the starting energy by the time through the pulling distance (Formula #4). As a general rule of thumb, higher power ratings mean less efficiency and less overall travel distance. A good mousetrap car that is designed for distance should have a low power rating.

**Power Output, Gear Ratio, Mechanical Advantage**

# Formulas

$$\text{Pulling Distance} = \text{Number of Turns} \times 2\pi r_{wheel}$$

$$\text{Number of Turns} = \frac{\text{Length of String}}{2\pi r_{axle}}$$

$$\text{Pulling Distance} = \frac{\text{Length of String} \times r_{wheel}}{r_{axle}}$$

$$P_1 = \frac{PE_{total}}{\Delta t_1}$$

Power is the rate at which energy is being used

**How it Works:**

*A caliper is used to measure the thickness of the drive axle in order to calculate the diameter. For a more accurate calculation of the diameter of the drive axle two measurements will be taken, without string and with string.*

CALIPER

REAR AXLE
WITH STRING
WOUND TIGHTLY

## Power Output, Gear Ratio, Mechanical Advantage

# Getting The Measurements

**Step 1:** Use a caliper or micrometer to measure and calculate the average diameter of the drive axle. Calculate the average diameter of the drive axle by first measuring the drive axle without string on it and then measuring it with string wound-up as it will normally be before a race. It is important that the string be wound evenly and not "balled" or "clumped." Add the two measurements together and then divide by 2. This will give you an average diameter for your calculations. Calculate the average radius from the average diameter.

Ave Drive Axle Diameter = _____ meters

Ave Drive Axle Radius = _____ meters

**Step 2:** Use a caliper or a ruler to measure the diameter of the drive wheel(s) and record the diameters as well as the radii.

Drive Wheel(s) Diameter = _____ meters

Drive Wheel(s) Radius = _____ meters

**Step 3:** Measure only the length of string that is normally pulled from the drive axle. Important: If there is more string attached to the lever arm than is needed, you may have to wind the string around the drive axle and then mark the string where it starts and ends with respect to the lever arm's travel range.

String Length = _____ meters

**Power Output, Gear Ratio, Mechanical Advantage**

THE PULLING DISTANCE IS THIS ...

**Step 4:** Calculate the pulling distance using the following formula:

$$\text{Pulling Distance} = \frac{\text{Length of String} \times r_{wheel}}{r_{axle}}$$

**Step 5:** Calculate the mechanical advantage from the following formula

$$\frac{F_{\text{Force string applies to drive axle}}}{F_{\text{Force of wheel to road}}} = \frac{r_{\text{radius of wheel}}}{r_{\text{radius of drive axle}}} = \frac{d_{\text{Distance vehicle is pulled by lever arm}}}{d_{\text{String on axle}}} = IMA$$

## Part II    Determine Power Output

**Step 6:** Time your vehicle over the pulling distance. Perform 3 to 5 trials. Record your data in the data table.

# Data Table #1

| Pulling Distance | Total Travel Distance | Time Over Pulling Distance | Starting Energy from Lab #2 | Power Output |
|---|---|---|---|---|
| $d_1=$ | Total $d_1=$ | $t_1=$ | PE $=$ | $P_1=$ |
| $d_2=$ | Total $d_2=$ | $t_2=$ | PE $=$ | $P_2=$ |
| $d_3=$ | Total $d_3=$ | $t_3=$ | PE $=$ | $P_3=$ |
| Ave $d=$ | | Ave $t=$ | | Ave $P=$ |

## Power Output, Gear Ratio, Mechanical Advantage

**Step 7:** Calculate the power by dividing the total starting energy from Lab #2 by the time over the pulling distance. Compare your value to other vehicles' power.

$$P_1 = \frac{PE_{total}}{\Delta t_1} \qquad P_2 = \frac{PE_{total}}{\Delta t_2}$$

## Graphing the Results

1. Make a graph of the **Power Rating** vs. **total travel distance**. Put "power" on the horizontal axis and "distance" on the vertical axis.
2. Make a graph of **Pulling Distance** vs. **Mechanical Advantage**. Put "mechanical advantage" on the horizontal axis and "pulling distance" on the vertical axis.

## Analysis

1. Describe any relationship that might exist between power rating and travel distance.
2. Describe any relationship that might exist between wheel to axle ratio and pulling distance.

**Power Output, Gear Ratio, Mechanical Advantage**

## Purpose

To determine the amount of rolling friction acting against your mousetrap car and the coefficient of friction.

## Materials

Ruler  (A caliper works better for smaller measurements.)
Smooth Ramp
Tape Measure

## Variables needed from other labs

Total Potential Energy from Lab #2

## Discussion

Friction is a force that acts against the motion of all moving objects. Energy is required to overcome friction and keep an object moving. Mousetrap cars start with a limited supply of energy. This energy is used to overcome friction and propel the vehicle. The less friction acting against a moving mousetrap car, the less energy that is consumed to friction and the further that the vehicle will travel. A moving mousetrap car is affected by two type of friction: airfriction and bearing friction. Airfriction is a large factor only with cars that are moving fast and is nearly negligible for slow-moving distance cars; therefore, in this lab you will only take bearing friction into consideration. Bearing friction is actually caused by two surfaces rubbing against one another. The amount of friction depends on the materials that are doing the rubbing and the force pressing them together (Formula #3). In this lab you will find the combined force of friction from all bearings on your vehicle. This combined frictional force will be called the rolling friction. The smaller the coefficient of friction, the more efficient your mousetrap car and the greater the travel distance will be.

**Rolling Friction, Work**

# The Set-up

Finding the theoretical rolling friction requires placing your mousetrap car on a smooth and flat board or ramp. The ramp will be elevated from one end slowly until your mousetrap car "JUST" begins to roll at constant velocity. This point or angle is where the force pulling the car down the ramp is equal to the force of rolling friction acting against the car (Formula #2). The force pulling the car down the ramp is a combination of two forces: the force of gravity pulling straight down and the normal force of the ramp pushing back (Formula #4). As the angle of the ramp is increased, the normal force decreases (Formula #5). The force of gravity remains unchanged for all angles. The difference between the two forces causes the force down the ramp to increase. The greater the angle required to move the car, the more friction there will be acting against the car's motion. The angle is directly proportional to the force of friction or the coefficient of rolling friction. **LOWER ANGLES** are more desirable (Formula #7).

**105**

### How it Works:
*The force pulling the vehicle down the ramp is equal to the force of friction acting against the car AS LONG as the mousetrap car moves down the ramp at a constant velocity. In some cases, once the vehicle starts to move the ramp has to be lowered in order to maintain constant velocity.*

**Rolling Friction, Work**

# Formulas

**Formula #1:** $\sum F = 0$

The sum of all forces must equal "zero" if there is no acceleration.

**Formula #2:** Force Pulling = Force of Friction

**Formula #3:** $f_{rf} = \mu N$

Force of friction is equal to the coefficient of friction times the normal force

$$\sin \theta = \frac{h}{L}$$

Because your measurements are from a slope, you will have to use some trigonometry

**Formula #4:** $f_{rf} = \sin \theta \cdot \text{w}$

The force down an angled ramp is equal to the force of friction as long as the vehicle rolls down the ramp with a constant velocity.

**Formula #5:** $N = \cos \theta \cdot \text{w}$

The normal force is the force that is perpendicularto the angled ramp.

**Formula #6:** $\mu = \dfrac{\sin \theta \cdot \text{w}}{\cos \theta \cdot \text{w}} = \tan \theta$

Resolving for the coefficient of friction from Formulas #3, #4 and #5

**Formula #7:** $\mu = \tan \theta$

The coefficient of friction

**Rolling Friction, Work**

# Trigonometry

Trigonometry is a fancy type of mathematics that is based on simple relationships of all right triangles. Ancient mathematicians found that all right triangles are proportional by ratios of their sides and angles. These ratios times the angle are known as sine, cosine, and tangent. Knowing one of the angles other than the right angle-and any one of the sides to the triangle-will allow you can calculate everything else you would ever need to know about that triangle's sides or angles.

107

### How it Works

*The angle of the ramp in this experiment forms a right triangle. The force due to gravity and the normal force of the ramp's surface cause a force directed down the ramp called "Force Down." These three forces form a right triangle which has the same angle as the base of the ramp. Knowing the angle of the base of the ramp and the weight of the car on the ramp, we can solve for any other force including the force acting down the ramp and which is equal to the force of friction.*

## Rolling Friction, Work

# Let The Good Times Roll

**Step 1:** Start by selecting a long and smooth board or ramp that will not bend or flex when lifted at one end. Your vehicle must fit on the ramp.

**Step 2:** Measure the length of the board and record this measurement as the board length (L).

**Step 3:** Place your vehicle on the ramp and begin lifting by one end. Slowly lift until the vehicle "JUST" begins to roll. Measure carefully and accurately the elevation of the board when the vehicle begins to roll and record this in the data table as the height (h). Repeat this process 5 to 10 times for more accurate results. (Note: You must subtract the thickness of the board from the height. Measure both ends of the ramp to correctly calculate the height.)

## Data Table #1

| Trial # | Board Length | Raised Height | Angle | Coefficient of Rolling Friction | Friction | Starting Energy | Predicted Travel Distance |
|---|---|---|---|---|---|---|---|
| 1 | L= | $h_1=$ | $\theta_1=$ | $\mu_1=$ | $f_1=$ | PE= | $d_1=$ |
| 2 | L= | $h_2=$ | $\theta_2=$ | $\mu_2=$ | $f_2=$ | PE= | $d_2=$ |
| 3 | L= | $h_3=$ | $\theta_3=$ | $\mu_3=$ | $f_3=$ | PE= | $d_3=$ |
| 4 | L= | $h_4=$ | $\theta_4=$ | $\mu_4=$ | $f_4=$ | PE= | $d_4=$ |
| AVE | | h= | $\theta=$ | $\mu=$ | f= | | d= |

**Rolling Friction, Work**

**Step 4:** Calculate the angle for each trial using the following equation:

$$\theta = \frac{h}{L} \sin^{-1}$$

**Step 5:** From the derived formula, calculate the coefficient of friction for each trial. The coefficient of friction is directly proportional to the angle of the ramp. Smaller angles translate into greater travel distance.

$$\mu = \tan\theta$$

**Step 6:** If this lab is performed correctly, the force of rolling friction acting against your car is equal to the force pulling the vehicle down the ramp in the elevated state. Calculate the force of friction by assuming that the force down the ramp is equal to the force of friction acting against the motion of your vehicle. Solve for the force down the ramp. MAKE SURE to use the weight of your vehicle in Newtons. If you have the mass, you can calculate the weight by multiplying the mass of your vehicle by 9.8 m/s$^2$ or find the weight by weighing your vehicle on a spring scale.

$$f_{rf} = \sin\theta \cdot w$$

**Step 7:** Using the starting energy that you calculated in Lab #2 you can calculate the predicted travel distance by using the following:

$$\text{Predicted Travel Distance} = \frac{\text{Total Potential Energy}}{\text{Rolling Friction}}$$

**Rolling Friction, Work**

## Background for Part 2:

# Predicting Travel Distance

Mousetrap cars convert their starting energy into work. Work is done to overcome the frictional forces acting against the vehicle. In most cases the largest amount of friction is the rolling friction caused by the bearings on the axles. If you know your starting energy and the rolling friction, you can make a rough prediction as to how far your car should travel. The total work that your car can do overcoming friction is equal to the starting energy that you calculated in Lab #2. The predicted travel distance is equal to the starting energy divided by the force of rolling friction. You should observe (by comparing your results to other students' results) that the less rolling friction that there is, the greater the distance a vehicle should travel.

**Formula #8:** $PE = f_{rf}d$

Work is equal to the starting energy.

**Formula #9:** $d = \dfrac{PE}{f_{rf}}$

The maximum distance depends on the starting energy and the force of rolling friction

## Rolling Friction, Work

# Calculate the Friction from the Actual Travel Distance

## Part #2

**Step 8:** Wind-up and release your vehicle. Measure the total travel distance. Test your result several times. Calculate the average travel distance for your vehicle.

## Data Table #2

| Trial # | Actual Travel Distance | Starting Energy | Friction | Coefficient of Rolling Friction |
|---------|------------------------|-----------------|----------|----------------------------------|
| 1 | $d_1=$ | PE= | $f_1=$ | $\mu_1=$ |
| 2 | $d_2=$ | PE= | $f_2=$ | $\mu_2=$ |
| 3 | $d_3=$ | PE= | $f_3=$ | $\mu_3=$ |
| 4 | $d_4=$ | PE= | $f_4=$ | $\mu_4=$ |
| AVE | $d=$ | | $f=$ | $\mu=$ |

**Step 9:** Calculate the rolling friction from the actual travel distance using the following formula:

$$\text{Work} = \text{Force} \cdot \text{Distance}$$

$$f_1 = \frac{PE_1}{d_1}$$

**Step 10:** Coefficient of sliding friction is a ratio of friction to normal force pressing against two surfaces. There are many variables that really affect the overall friction acting against a mousetrap car including air resistance. Air resistance is only a large force a vehicle is moving fast. If your vehicle is a slow mover, the amount of air resistance will be rather small. We are going to calculate the coefficient of friction assuming that the

## Rolling Friction, Work

only friction acting on a mousetrap car is the rolling friction of the bearings and not air resistance. Calculate the coefficient of friction from the following formula. Note: For mass use only the mass of the frame without the wheels. It is the frame that rests on the bearings and presses the bearings' surfaces together. Therefore, you must remove the wheels and "mass" only the frame.

$$\mu = \frac{f}{mg}$$

## Graphing the Results

1. Make a graph of **Coefficient of Friction** vs. **Travel Distance** from all other vehicles in the class. Put the coefficient of friction from Part 1 on the horizontal axis and travel distance on the vertical axis.

## Analysis

1. Explain why your observed results might be different than those of your predicted travel distance.

2. Explain which coefficient of friction calculated, Part 1 or Part 2, is more accurate and why.

**Rolling Friction, Work**

# Lab #5 - As The Wheels Turn

## Purpose
In this activity you will find the rotational inertia of your wheels.

## Materials
A Small Mass (no larger than 50g)
Stopwatch
String
Meter Stick
Pulley Set-up

## Discussion
Rotational inertia is the resistance an object has to changing its state of rotation. The more rotational inertia a wheel has, the more torque that will be required to change its state of rotation. The torque is generated from the mousetrap's lever arm. More torque means shorter lever arms which translates into less pulling distance. With distance cars you want the longest possible pulling distance; therefore, you want a long lever arms. In most cases, whether you are building a speed or distance car it is best to have wheels with as little rotational inertia as possible. The less rotational inertia that a wheel has, the easier it will be to

*Just as an object at rest tends to stay at rest and an object in motion tends to stay in motion, an object in a state of rotation about an axis tends to remain in that state of rotation about the same axis unless an external force or torque acts on it. Try an experiment to learn about rotational inertia. Try twisting a barbell with the weight spaced close together and then far apart. You will definitely get a good feel for rotational inertia after this experiment.*

**Rotational Inertia**

# The Set-up

accelerate the wheel and get the car moving. Rotational inertia is equal to the amount of torque acting on a system divided be the angular acceleration (Formula #1). The angular acceleration is equal to the linear acceleration divided by the radius of the wheel (Formula #2). The torque is equal to the applied force times the radius from the point of rotation (Formula #3). Putting Formula #1, #2 and #3 together you get Formula #4.

In this lab a weight is tied to a string and then wrapped around the axle of each wheel. The weight is allowed to fall causing the wheel(s) to spin. As the weight falls it is also timed. Based on the time it takes the weight to reach the tabletop or floor, you can calculate the rotational resistance of your wheel(s). The weight, as it falls, is being pulled downwards by gravity and upwards by the resistance of the wheel(s). The greater the rotational resistance or inertia, the longer it will take the weight to fall. The acceleration of the falling weight is found by Formula #5. Combine Formula #4 and #5 to get one formula that will be used for this lab to calculate the rotational inertia, based on the time of fall for the hanging mass. The total rotational inertia is the combination of all wheels added together.

115

**Rotational Inertia**

> *In this lab a weight is tied to a string and then wound around an axle. Based on the time it takes the weight to reach the tabletop or floor, you can calculate the rotational resistance of your wheel(s). The greater the rotational resistance or inertia, the longer it will take the weight to fall.*

I = Rotational Inertia
$\tau$ = Torque
$\alpha$ = Angular Acceleration
a = Linear Acceleration
F = Applied Force
r = Lever Length
h = Fall Height of Mass
$v_0$ = Starting Falling Velocity  (zero in this lab)
t = Time of Fall for Mass
a = Linear Acceleration

# Formulas

**Formula #1:**    $\tau = Fr$

**Formula #2:**    $I = \dfrac{\tau}{\alpha}$

**Formula #3:**    $\alpha = \dfrac{a}{r}$

Angular acceleration based on linear acceleration

**Formula #4:**    $I = \dfrac{Fr}{\dfrac{a}{r}}$

Formulas 1 - 3 combined

**Formula #5:**    $I = \dfrac{Fr^2}{a}$

Rotational inertia from Formula #3 based on linear acceleration

**Formula #6:**    $h = v_o t + \dfrac{1}{2}at^2$

The height of fall based on an accelerating object through time

**Formula #7:**    $a = \dfrac{2h}{t^2}$

Solving for acceleration

## Rotational Inertia

**Formula #8:** $I = \dfrac{Fr^2 t^2}{2h}$

Rotational inertia of a wheel based on a falling mass

# Another Way to Get The Job Done

If your wheel(s) is (are) not glued to the axle, then you may have to design a test device to hold and measure the rotational inertia. Design a pulley apparatus that can hold each of your wheels and that will allow them to spin freely. The smaller the pulley or axle that the string is wrapped around, the smaller the acceleration of the falling mass, which makes timing more accurate.

CLAMP HELD
TO A RING STAND

REAR AXLE

TAPPERED
CONE

BEARING

CLAY

MASS

**Rotational Inertia**

**How it Works:**
*In this set-up an axle is mounted in a bearing. The bearing is held to a ringstand by a clamp. A tapered cone is attached to one end of the axle. The wheel is placed onto the tapered cone and then held in place with a small amount of clay. The string is wrapped around the opposite side of the axle.*

# Let's Get Spinning

**IMPORTANT:** Steps 1-5 are only for those who test their wheels on a pulley sytem. If you art measuring your wheels' rotational inertia on your vehicle's axles, then skip to Step 6.

## Finding the rotational inertia of the pulley set-up

**Step 1:** Because the pulley set-up has rotational inertia of its own you will have to calculate its rotational inertia in order to subtract it from that of your wheel. Make the following data table:

## Data Table #1

| Fall Distance of Mass | Time of Fall | Radius of Pulley | Weight of Falling Mass | Rotational Inertia of Pulley |
|---|---|---|---|---|
| $d_1 =$ | $t_1 =$ | $r_p =$ | $W =$ | $I_{pulley\ 1} =$ |
| $d_2 =$ | $t_2 =$ | $r_p =$ | $W =$ | $I_{pulley\ 2} =$ |
| $d_3 =$ | $t_3 =$ | $r_p =$ | $W =$ | $I_{pulley\ 3} =$ |
| $d_4 =$ | $t_4 =$ | $r_p =$ | $W =$ | $I_{pulley\ 4} =$ |
| AVE | $t =$ | | $W =$ | $I_{pulley} =$ |

**Step 2:** Calculate the weight of your hanging mass by dividing grams by 1000 and then multiping by 9.8. This will give you weight in Newtons. Record in the data table as W. It is best to use a smaller mass no larger than 50g. I suggest 20g. Attach the weight to the end of a string that is long enough to reach from the pulley to the floor or table top, depending on the fall distance that you will use for your measurement. Attach the other end of the string to the axle or pulley set-up and wind the string up around your setup.

**Step 3:** Measure the fall distance from the bottom of the hanging weight to the surface below and record this measurement as fall distance of mass (d). Measure the radius of the axle or pulley where the string is wound and record as the pulley radius (r).

**Rotational Inertia**

**Step 4:** Allow the weight to fall while timing with a stopwatch and record the time in the data table (t). Repeat several times and record in the Data Table #1. Find an average. Make sure that you drop the weight from the same point each time that you repeat the experiment.

**Step 5:** Using the following formula, calculate the rotational inertia of your pulley.

$$I = \frac{Fr^2t^2}{2h}$$

$I_{\text{Rotational Inertia of pulley}} = \frac{(\text{Weight of Hanging Mass}) * (\text{Radius of Pully})^2 * (\text{Time of Fall})^2}{2 * (\text{Distance that mass falls})}$

## Finding the rotational inertia of your wheels

**Step 6:** Depending on whether you will measure each wheel by itself or if you will measure the rotational inertia of an axle system, make a copy of Data Table #2 for each wheel or axle sysetm for your vehicle. If you had to perform steps 1-5 then record the average rotational inertia from your pulley set-up in Data Table #2.

## Data Table #2   (Front Axle System or Wheel #1)

| Fall Distance of Mass | Time of Fall | Radius of Pulley | Weight of Falling Mass | Rotational Inertia of Pulley | Rotational Inertia of Wheel |
|---|---|---|---|---|---|
| $d_1=$ | $t_1=$ | $r_p=$ | $W=$ | $I_{pulley}=$ | $I_{wheel\ 1}=$ |
| $d_2=$ | $t_2=$ | $r_p=$ | $W=$ | $I_{pulley}=$ | $I_{wheel\ 2}=$ |
| $d_3=$ | $t_3=$ | $r_p=$ | $W=$ | $I_{pulley}=$ | $I_{wheel\ 3}=$ |
| $d_4=$ | $t_4=$ | $r_p=$ | $W=$ | $I_{pulley}=$ | $I_{wheel\ 4}=$ |
| AVE | $t=$ | | | | $I_{wheel}=$ |

## Rotational Inertia

**Step 7:** Attach one wheel at a time to the pulley apparatus if you are measuring each wheel by itself. If you are measuring a complete axle system, then perform the following:

Attach one end of a string to the axle and the other end of a weight. The string should be long enough to reach the surface below. Calculate the weight of your hanging mass by dividing grams by 1000 and then multiping by 9.8. This will give you weight in Newtons. Record in the data table as W. It is best to use a smaller mass no larger than 50g. I suggest 20g. Wind the string around the axle and measure the starting possition of the mass so that in all trials the mass falls from the same height.

**Step 8:** Allow the weight to fall while timing with a stopwatch and record the time in the data table (t). Repeat several times and record in the Data Table #2. Find an average. Make sure that you drop the weight from the same point each time that you repeat the experiment.

## Rotational Inertia

**Step 9:** Using the following formula, calculate the rotational inertia of your wheel. Look carefully at the formula. It is the same as in Step 5 except this time you have to remove the rotational inertial of the pulley. Do not forget to subtract the resistance inertia of the pulley.! If you did not use a pulley set-up ignore the rotatioanl inertia of the pulley and plug in all varibles except for the rotational inertia of the pulley.

### Rotational Inertia of a Wheel or an Axle System

$$I_{\text{Rotational Inertia of Wheel}} = \frac{(\text{Weight of Hanging Mass}) * (\text{Radius of Pully})^2 * (\text{Time of Fall})^2}{2 * (\text{Distance that mass falls})} - I_{\text{Pulley}}$$

**Step 10:** Repeat for each wheel or axle system of your car and record your results in Data Table #3 as follows: "Front Wheel #1," "Rear Wheel #2," or "Front Axle system," "Rear Axle system" .

## Data Table #3

|  | Front Wheel #1 Or Front Axle System | Front Wheel #2 | Rear Wheel #1 Or Rear Axle System | Rear Wheel #2 |
|---|---|---|---|---|
| Rotational Inertia | $I_{f1}=$ | $I_{f2}=$ | $I_{r1}=$ | $I_{r2}=$ |
| Radius of Wheel | $r_{f1}=$ | $r_{f2}=$ | $r_{r1}=$ | $r_{r2}=$ |

**Step 11:** Add the rotational inertia for all components together in order to get the total rotational inertia.

Total Rotational Inertia = _____ kg • m$^2$

### Rotational Inertia

# Lab #6 - Conserving Energy

## Purpose
In this activity you will calculate the efficiency of your mousetrap car

## Materials
Ruler
Caliper
Stopwatch

## Variables needed from other labs
Total Potential Energy from Lab #2
Rolling Friction from Lab #4
Coefficient of Rolling Friction from Lab #4
Rotational Inertia for each Wheel or Axle System from Lab #5

## Discussion
In this lab you will calculate the overall efficiency of your vehicle. Efficiency is how effectively a machine can transform energy into work without losing energy to friction. It is a rule of nature that in all transformations of energy some energy will be lost to the surroundings because of friction. More efficient machines lose less energy to friction. Efficiency allows you to see just how much of your energy is being used as designed. A mousetrap car uses energy to change speed and displace its position. With a slow-moving distance car, you would expect a more efficient vehicle to travel further than a less efficient car. With a distance car the objective is to reduce friction to a minimum, thereby increasing distance to a maximum.

With a speed car, the objective is to quickly transform the stored potential energy into energy of motion. For a speed car you can measure the efficiency by comparing the starting potential energy to the ending kinetic energy as

**Conservation of Energy**

# Lets Get Rolling

the vehicle crosses the finish line. The kinetic energy will be stored in two forms: rotational kinetic energy and linear kinetic energy. Rotational kinetic energy is the energy that is in the rotation of the wheels. Linear kinetic energy is in the movement of the car. These two forms of kinetic energy have to be calculated independently and then added together in order to find the total energy at the finish.

## Finding the Rolling Friction

**Step 1:** Use the information from Lab # 2 and record your mousetrap cars starting potential energy .

Total Starting Energy = _____ Joules

## Data Table #1

| Pulling Distance | Time | Final Velocity | Linear Kinetic Energy | Total Rotational Energy | Total Kinetic Energy | Work Done | Efficiency |
|---|---|---|---|---|---|---|---|
| $d_1 =$ | $t_1 =$ | $v_1 =$ | $KE_{tran\ 1} =$ | $KE_{rot\ 1} =$ | $KE_1 =$ | $w_1 =$ | $E_1 =$ |
| $d_2 =$ | $t_2 =$ | $v_2 =$ | $KE_{tran\ 2} =$ | $KE_{rot\ 2} =$ | $KE_2 =$ | $w_2 =$ | $E_2 =$ |
| $d_3 =$ | $t_3 =$ | $v_3 =$ | $KE_{tran\ 3} =$ | $KE_{rot\ 3} =$ | $KE_3 =$ | $w_3 =$ | $E_3 =$ |
| $d_4 =$ | $t_4 =$ | $v_4 =$ | $KE_{tran\ 4} =$ | $KE_{rot\ 4} =$ | $KE_4 =$ | $w_4 =$ | $E_4 =$ |
| AVE | $d =$ | $h =$ | $KE_{tran} =$ | $KE_{rot} =$ | $KE =$ | $w =$ | $E =$ |

**Step 2:** Place your mousetrap car on the start line  Walk along side of your mousetrap car and measure the pulling distance. You can also use the data you calculated from Lab #3: *Predicting Pulling Distance*. Record the pulling distance in Data Table #1 under "Pulling Distance. "

## Conservation of Energy

**Step 3:** Place your mousetrap car on the start line. Release the mousetrap car and time it over the pulling distance only. **Do not time beyond the pulling distance**. Test three to five times and record in Data Table #1 under "Time."

**Step 4:** Use the following formula to calculate the final velocities for each trial. Record your results in Data Table #1 under "Final velocity."

$$\text{Final Velocity} = \frac{2 * \text{Pulling Distance}}{\text{Time}}$$

**Step 5:** Find the mass for your vehicle so that you can calculate the linear kinetic energy. Calculate the linear kinetic energy for each trial using the mass times the final velocity squared. Record your answer under "Linear Kinetic Energy" in Data Table #1.

$$KE_{tran_1} = \frac{(m) * (V_{f_1})^2}{2}$$

## Finding the Rotational Kinetic Energy

**Step 6:** From Lab#5 record the rotational inertia for each wheel or axle system in data table #2. Aslo record the radius for each wheel on your vehicle.

## Data Table #2

|  | Front Wheel #1 Or Front Axle System | Front Wheel #2 | Rear Wheel #1 Or Rear Axle System | Rear Wheel #2 |
|---|---|---|---|---|
| **Rotational Inertia** | $I_{f1} =$ | $I_{f2} =$ | $I_{r1} =$ | $I_{r2} =$ |
| **Radius of Wheel** | $r_{f1} =$ | $r_{f2} =$ | $r_{r1} =$ | $r_{r2} =$ |

**Conservation of Energy**

**Step 7:** Using the final velocities from Table #1, calculate the rotational kinetic energy for each trial. You must calculate each wheel or axle system separately.

$$KE\,1_{rot\,1} = \frac{(I_1) * (v_{f1})^2}{2*(r_1)^2}$$

## Data Table #3

| Trial # | $KE_{rot}$ Wheel #1 | $KE_{rot}$ Wheel #2 | $KE_{rot}$ Wheel #3 | $KE_{rot}$ Wheel #4 | Total Rotational Kinetic Energy |
|---------|---------|---------|---------|---------|-------------------|
| 1= | KE $1_{rot\,1}$= | KE $2_{rot\,1}$= | KE $3_{rot\,1}$= | KE $4_{rot\,1}$= | KE $_{rot\,1}$= |
| 2= | KE $1_{rot\,2}$= | KE $2_{rot\,2}$= | KE $3_{rot\,2}$= | KE $4_{rot\,2}$= | KE $_{rot\,2}$= |
| 3= | KE $1_{rot\,3}$= | KE $2_{rot\,3}$= | KE $3_{rot\,3}$= | KE $4_{rot\,3}$= | KE $_{rot\,3}$= |
| 4= | KE $1_{rot\,4}$= | KE $2_{rot\,4}$= | KE $3_{rot\,4}$= | KE $4_{rot\,4}$= | KE $_{rot\,4}$= |
| | | | | | |

**Step 8:** Once you have found the rotational kinetic energy for each wheel, add each value together for each trial in order to get the total rotational kinetic energy, record in Data Table #3 and then transfer the Total Rotational Kinetic Energy to Table #1.

$$KE_{rot_1} = KE\,1_{rot_1} + KE\,2_{rot_1} + KE\,3_{rot_1} + KE\,4_{rot_1}$$

**Step 9:** From Table #1 add the linear kinetic energy with the total rotational kinetic energy. This value represents the total energy of your vehicle when all the potential energy is converted into kinetic energy.

$$KE_1 = KE_{rot_1} + KE_{tran_1}$$

## Conservation of Energy

**Step 10:** Subtract the total kinetic energy from the starting potential energy to get the work lost to friction.

$$W_1 = PE_1 - KE_1$$

**Step 11:** With a distance vehicle the objective is to convert the starting potential energy into distance by doing work to overcome friction. With a speed car the objective is to convert the starting potential energy into kinetic energy. Calculate the efficiency for your vehicle by dividing the total kinetic energy by the starting potential energy and then multiplying by 100 in order to get a percentage.

$$Efficiency_1 = \frac{KE_1}{PE_{start}} * 100$$

**Step 12:** Calculate the amount of rolling friction acting against your vehicle using the energy lost to friction or the work divided by the pulling distance.

$$f_1 = \frac{W_1}{d_1}$$

**Conservation of Energy**

# Graphing the Results

You will now graph your data in order to learn from your results. In each of the following graphs, attempt to draw a "best fit" line. If data is widely scattered, do not attempt to connect each dot but instead draw the best line you can that represents the shape of the dots. If you have access to a computer, you can use a spread sheet like Microsoft Exel to plot your data.

1. Graph **Pulling Distance** vs. **Work** for each vehicle in the class.

2. Graph **Pulling Distance** vs **Efficiency** for each vehicle in the class.

# Analysis

1. Explain how pulling distance is related to energy lost to friction or the work done.

2. Explain the relationship that exists between pulling distance and efficiency.

## OBJECTIVE:

Build a vehicle powered solely by the energy of one standard-sized mouse trap (1 3/4" X 3 7/8") that will travel the greatest linear distance.

By definition, a vehicle is "a device with wheels or runners used to carry something (e.g., car, bus, bicycle or sled)." Therefore, launching a ball (e.g., marble) from the mouse trap will be ruled illegal.

## REGULATIONS:

1. The device must be powered by a single "Victor" brand mouse trap (1 3/4" X 3 7/8"). Other brands may be used if permitted.
2. The mouse trap can not be physically altered except for the following: 4 holes can be drilled only to mount the mouse trap to the frame and a mouse-trap's spring can be removed only to adjust the length of its lever arm.
3. The device cannot have any additional potential or kinetic energy at the start other than what can be stored in the mouse-trap's spring itself. (This also means that you cannot push start your vehicle.)
4. The spring from the mouse trap cannot be altered or heat treated.
5. The spring cannot be wound more than its normal travel distance or 180 degrees.
6. Vehicles must be self-starting. Vehicles may not receive a push in the forward direction or side direction.
7. The vehicle must steer itself. Measurements of distance will not measure the total distance travele,d only the displacement distance.
8. Distance will be measured from the front of the tape at the starting line to the point of the vehicle that was closest to the start line at the time of release.
9. The instructor has the final decision as to the appropriateness of any additional items that might be used in the construction of the vehicle.

## RUNNING THE CONTEST:

1. The race track can be any smooth level floor, a gymnasium or a non-carpeted hallway.
2. Each contestant will be given three attempts. The winner will be that vehicle which has obtained the greatest distance on any one of the three attempts. Any ties will be decided by a single run-off between the vehicles which tied.

# Distance Contest Scoring

| | | | |
|---|---|---|---|
| 0 0 - 0 . 9 9 | meters | 5 | % |
| 0 1 - 0 1 . 9 9 | meters | 1 0 | % |
| 0 2 - 0 2 . 9 9 | meters | 1 5 | % |
| 0 3 - 0 3 . 9 9 | meters | 2 0 | % |
| 0 4 - 0 4 . 9 9 | meters | 2 5 | % |
| 0 5 - 0 5 . 9 9 | meters | 3 0 | % |
| 0 6 - 0 6 . 9 9 | meters | 3 5 | % |
| 0 7 - 0 7 . 9 9 | meters | 4 0 | % |
| 0 8 - 0 8 . 9 9 | meters | 4 5 | % |
| 0 9 - 0 9 . 9 9 | meters | 5 0 | % |
| 1 0 - 1 0 . 9 9 | meters | 5 5 | % |
| 1 1 - 1 1 . 9 9 | meters | 6 0 | % |
| 1 2 - 1 2 . 9 9 | meters | 6 5 | % |
| 1 3 - 1 3 . 9 9 | meters | 7 0 | % |
| 1 4 - 1 4 . 9 9 | meters | 7 5 | % |
| 1 5 - 1 5 . 9 9 | meters | 8 0 | % |
| 1 6 - 1 6 . 9 9 | meters | 8 5 | % |
| 1 7 - 1 7 . 9 9 | meters | 9 0 | % |
| 1 8 - 1 8 . 9 9 | meters | 9 5 | % |
| 1 9 - 1 9 . 9 9 | meters | 1 0 0 % | |
| 2 0 - 2 0 . 9 9 | meters | 1 0 5 % | |
| 2 1 - 2 1 . 9 9 | meters | 1 1 0 % | |
| 2 2 - 2 2 . 9 9 | meters | 1 1 5 % | |
| 2 3 - 2 3 . 9 9 | meters | 1 2 0 % | |

## OBJECTIVE:

Build a vehicle, powered solely by the energy of one standard-sized mouse trap (1 3/4" X 3 7/8") that will travel a 5-meter linear distance in the shortest amount of time.

By definition, a vehicle is "a device with wheels or runners used to carry something (e.g., a car, bus, bicycle, or sled)." Therefore, launching a ball (e.g., a marble) from the mouse trap will be ruled illegal.

## REGULATIONS:

1. The device must be powered by a single "Victor" brand mouse trap (1 3/4" X 3 7/8") Other brands may be used if permitted.
2. The mouse trap can not be physically altered except for the following: 4 holes can be drilled only to mount the mouse trap to the frame and a mouse-trap's spring can be removed only to adjust the length of its lever arm.
3. The device cannot have any additional potential or kinetic energy at the start other than what can be stored in the mouse-trap's spring itself. (This also means that you cannot push start your vehicle.)
4. The spring from the mouse trap cannot be altered or heat treated.
5. The spring cannot be wound more than its normal travel distance or 180 degrees.
6. Vehicles must be self-starting. Vehicles may not receive a push in the forward direction or side direction.
7. The vehicle must steer itself. Measurements of distance will not measure the total distance traveled, only the displacement distance.
8. Vehicles can not recieve a running start and must start as close as posible to the start line. Time of run will begin when any part of the vehicle passes over the start line and will ends when that same point passes over the 5-meter mark.
9. The instructor has the final decision as to the appropriateness of any additional items that might be used in the construction of the vehicle.

**130**

## RUNNING THE CONTEST:

1. The race track can be any smooth level floor, a gymnasium or a non-carpeted hallway.
2. Each contestant will be given three attempts. The winner will be that vehicle which has obtained the least time on any one of the three attempts. Any ties will be decided by a single run-off between the vehicle which tied.

# Speed Contest Scoring

| | | | |
|---|---|---|---|
| 7.25 - 7.49 | Seconds | 5 | % |
| 7.00 - 7.24 | Seconds | 10 | % |
| 6.75 - 6.99 | Seconds | 15 | % |
| 6.50 - 6.74 | Seconds | 20 | % |
| 6.25 - 6.49 | Seconds | 25 | % |
| 6.00 - 6.24 | Seconds | 30 | % |
| 5.75 - 5.99 | Seconds | 35 | % |
| 5.50 - 5.74 | Seconds | 40 | % |
| 5.25 - 5.49 | Seconds | 45 | % |
| 5.00 - 5.24 | Seconds | 50 | % |
| 4.75 - 4.99 | Seconds | 55 | % |
| 4.50 - 4.74 | Seconds | 60 | % |
| 4.25 - 4.49 | Seconds | 65 | % |
| 4.00 - 4.24 | Seconds | 70 | % |
| 3.75 - 3.99 | Seconds | 75 | % |
| 3.50 - 3.74 | Seconds | 80 | % |
| 3.25 - 3.49 | Seconds | 85 | % |
| 3.00 - 3.24 | Seconds | 90 | % |
| 2.75 - 2.99 | Seconds | 95 | % |
| 2.50 - 2.74 | Seconds | 100 | % |
| 2.25 - 2.49 | Seconds | 105 | % |
| 2.00 - 2.24 | Seconds | 110 | % |
| 1.75 - 1.99 | Seconds | 115 | % |
| 1.50 - 1.74 | Seconds | 120 | % |

# Just for Fun

*If you like excitement in your life, then this is for you. This is the best game I have ever seen. It is called Perfect Timing!™ Two physics teachers developed it with the help of their students. It is the only game where people play against one another with a stopwatch. My students love it! I cannot get them to stop playing and feel sure this is bound to be the next mega-hit game. This is one of the few products that I am proud to recommend.*

Is time on your side? **Perfect Timing!**™ is the split-second stopwatch game that will challenge your perception of time and drive you crazy! Players of **Perfect Timing!**™ estimate time on a stopwatch and compare their times to each other during "*Race Against Time*" challenges. Whoever has the "best of times" will be the winner and earn a *Time-Saver* card. Those with the "worst of times" will lose precious time from their timelines. Run out of time and you will be sent to Time Out. In order to win at **Perfect Timing!**™ you must control your time and be the first to collect all ten *Time-Saver* cards before your time is up. The action is intense and non-stop. Everybody plays continuously. Players must develop strategies and make rapid decisions or the game will be over quickly, because "time waits for no one."

**Perfect Timing!**™ It's not just another "bored" game!

# Perfect Timing!

## The Stopwatch Game

# Cotmer Productions

**P.O. Box 27**
**McNeil, TX 78651**

**(512) 238-7445**

**http://www.cotmer.com**